The Maternal Face of God?

Explorations in Catholic Sophiology

ISTVÁN CSELÉNYI

The Maternal Face of God?

*Explorations in
Catholic Sophiology*

⊕

Preface by
Miklós Beer
Diocesan Bishop, Vác (Hungary)

Foreword by
Michael Martin

*God created man in the image of himself,
in the image of God created him, male
and female he created them.* (Gen 1:27)

ANGELICO PRESS
SOPHIA PERENNIS

First published in English in the USA
by Angelico Press/Sophia Perennis 2017
© István Cselényi 2017
Foreword © Michael Martin 2017
Preface © Miklós Beer 2017
Translation © Angelico Press 2017
Original Title: *Isten anyai arca? Egy hipotézis nyomában*
Budapest, 2007 © Mozaik Nyomda
Maternal Face of God? In Trace of an Hypothesis
Budapest, 2008 © Mozaik Nyomda

Translated by Bulcsú Hoppal,
Attila Tárnok, Bence Bíró

For information, address:
Angelico Press
4709 Briar Knoll Dr.
Kettering, OH 45429
angelicopress.com

ISBN 978 1 62138 242 3 pb
ISBN 978 1 62138 243 0 cloth
ISBN 978 1 62138 244 7 ebook

Cover image: *Holy Wisdom* icon, Russian, c. 1600
(wood, gesso, tempera)
Cover design: Michael Schrauzer

CONTENTS

ILLUSTRATIONS

Foreword

The (Re)Arrival of
Sophiology in the West

U NTIL relatively recently, sophiology was almost entirely ignored by Western theologians. And when it was not ignored,
it was treated as highly suspect. While not neglected in the
Orthodox East, particularly in Russia and among Russian theologians in the diaspora, sophiology was nonetheless regarded as theologically questionable and, indeed, heretical. In the early 20th
century, Fr. Sergius Bulgakov, the architect of Russian sophiology
and now regarded as one of the great theologians of modern Orthodoxy, was repeatedly attacked for his sophiology, and eventually cen-
sured by his Church.

The modern West learned about sophiology from the Russians
(Pavel Florensky and Vladimir Solovyov in addition to Bulgakov);
the influence of which is palpable in the theological aesthetics of
Hans Urs von Balthasar and in the Mariology of Louis Bouyer, to
name only the most obvious examples.[1] But, despite the invariably-
repeated romantic reveries gushing about the churches dedicated to
Holy Wisdom in early Russian Orthodoxy in the various excava-
tions of its historical record, sophiology is at its core a Western phenomenon; and, to add a note of irony, it is originally a Protestant
phenomenon, as its fountainhead is the Silesian Lutheran cobbler

---

1. Among others, see the section on von Balthasar in my *The Submerged Reality:
Sophiology and the Turn to a Poetic Metaphysics* (Kettering, OH: Angelico Press,
2015) as well as Jennifer Newsome Martin's essay "True and Truer *Gnosis*: The Rev-
elation of the Sophianic in Hans Urs von Balthasar" in *The Heavenly Country: An
Anthology of Primary Sources, Poetry, and Critical Essays on Sophiology*, ed. Michael
Martin (Kettering, OH: Angelico Press, 2016), 339–53.

Jakob Boehme. Boehme did for Western mysticism what Martin Heidegger later did for Western philosophy: he tore it down and began anew. And Boehme's sophiology is an integral part of that re-imagination. In a very real sense, as István Cselényi argues in the present volume, Boehme provides Catholic (and Orthodox) theology with a courageous and vigorous Mariology, a gift that has been for the most part left unopened (it has been, not surprisingly, uniformly rejected by mainstream Protestant theology). During the 17th century, Boehme's sophiology inspired the Philadelphian Society (John Pordage, Jane Lead, and Thomas Bromley, being the most noted) as well as German Pietism. In the 19th century his influence gradually reached Russia and Solovyov, the first of the Russian sophiologists. Nevertheless, it is only in the last decade or so that sophiology as such has been taken up with any theological *gravitas* in the West (and not subsumed into a larger argument as it is in von Balthasar and, to a lesser degree, in Bouyer).

An important moment in this rearrival of sophiology in the West is certainly John Milbank's seminal essay "Sophiology and Theurgy: The New Theological Horizon," in which he not only contextualizes sophiology in terms of Western theology but also resets a sophiological ontology contra what can only be called our current postmodern nominalism. For Milbank, this is nowhere more evident than in the ontology of gender and he encourages us to "link gender equality to the equality of Bride with Bridegroom, thereby not abandoning the essential significance of Biblical engendered typology, nor the Biblical and theological significance of sexual difference,"[2] an essential quality, I would argue, of sophiology, which is in its essence both a philosophy and a theology mindful of the Creator's presence in Creation. Fr. Alexis van der Mensbrugghe, a former Benedictine who had converted to Orthodoxy, had argued as much in his little-known treatise *From Dyad to Triad: A Plea against Duality and an Essay toward the Synthesis of Orthodoxy*, succinctly proposing that

---

2. John Milbank, "Sophiology and Theurgy: The New Theological Horizon" in *Encounter between Eastern Orthodoxy and Radical Orthodoxy*, ed. Adrian Pabst and Christoph Schneider (Farnham, UK: Ashgate, 2009), 45–85, at 83.

"the Man-Woman Dyad answers the God-Wisdom Dyad." [3] Mensbrugghe wrote these words in 1935, however: a time when the issue could hardly have seemed pressing or even controversial, least of all in the public square. Indeed, now, at a cultural moment Milbank presciently anticipated and that Mensbrugghe would have viewed with abject horror, Fr. István Cselényi, a Byzantine Catholic priest from Hungary, argues forcefully along the same lines, grounding an ontology of sexual difference in a thoroughly Catholic sophiology.

Throughout his book, in addition to offering insight into the work of "canonical" sophiologists such as Boehme and the Russians, Cselényi also investigates some previously unexplored avenues of sophiological insight in ontotheology, phenomenology, the Fathers, and Scholasticism. He further provides a provocative chapter on the sophiology at work in the thought of Carl Gustav Jung before arriving at his measured (if somewhat startling) argument that there may indeed be warrant to consider the Holy Spirit the *Sophia Increata,* the Uncreated Wisdom of God. Again and again, Cselényi emphasizes the nuptial, hierogamic nature of God's relationship to Creation, and it is upon this foundation that his sophiology rests. As he writes, "This nuptial-like relation is reflected on a small scale in all beings as the relation of matter and form, potential and act, the orders of substance and being, and as the duality and unity of body and soul in man, and further as the relationship of man and woman: marriage and family, on the level of interpersonal relations."[4] Indeed, *The Maternal Face of God?* could not have appeared at a more important time, as throughout its pages Fr. Cselényi makes the compelling case for a theology that articulates a clear and refreshing understanding of the relationship of the Divine Feminine to the Trinity and an ontology that affirms the goodness of Creation (Gen 1) and warns of the danger inherent to the cultural, ontological, and theological amnesia that has brought the human race to such a profoundly disturbing moment. He offers us an antidote to

3. Alexis van der Mensbrugghe, *From Dyad to Triad: A Plea against Duality and an Essay toward the Synthesis of Orthodoxy* (London: The Faith Press, 1935), 26.
4. See page 192.

this poison, for that is what sophiology is. Its rearrival could not have come at a more important moment.

"Thou art beautiful, O my love, sweet and comely as Jerusalem: terrible as an army set in array." (Song of Songs 6:3)

MICHAEL MARTIN
Pentecost 2016

Preface

Rembrandt: *Returning of the Prodigal Son*, 1663

ALMOST everyone knows Rembrandt's famous painting of the Prodigal Son. Many have noticed that the two hands lying on the back of the repentant son are different: one is fatherly, manly; the other, softer, caressing, motherly. In this way the painting shows us the two hands, the two sides, of the God of the Gospels: encompassing both paternal and maternal roles. This was what Pope John Paul I's well-known phrase also expressed: "God is Father—and even more, He is Mother." Now, in the year of Divine Mercy, we are especially receptive to signs, notions, and suggestions of this sort.

The present book leads us into this system of signs. My classmate in seminary, the author of this book, Fr. István Cselényi, has for decades been studying the question: Are there maternal attributes to God? *God's Maternal Face?* (written with the question mark) was the title of his book published on the topic in 2007 in Hungarian, which was translated into English the following year. We have in our hands the second edition of his work. Here, too, he seeks only to pose questions. He ventures to reflect upon the hypothesis that there are indications in nature, human existence, and most importantly, in revelation, which hint at this possibility.

He finds that we can experience dualities and their unity everywhere in the structure of nature. Man carries the duality of body and soul, and the pivotal point of interpersonal relations is the love-bond between man and woman. He sees at the root of this the fact that God created man in His image as man and woman (Gen 1:27). Hence it may be that both masculinity and femininity were present even in the "archetype." He finds support for this view already in the Old Testament—for example, in the concept of Divine Wisdom (Sophia) and Spirit (*Ruah*, Yahweh).

Additionally, in the New Testament he highlights certain moments that we tend to overlook, such as the Baptism of the Lord Jesus, when the Holy Spirit descended upon Him in the form of a mother dove (*peristera*) (Matt 3:13–17 and its parallels), or that the Spirit for us is the Spirit of Rebirth (John 3:5)—i.e., the Holy Spirit gives birth to us on a new, supernatural plane of existence and teaches, edifies, guides us on the way to the fullness of truth as a watchful mother. The book also reveals that several authors writing on spirituality and mysticism promoted the notion of this "maternal character" (e.g., St. Hildegard of Bingen, Jakob Boehme, and Russian theosophist Vladimir Solovyov).

In this new edition the author also addresses possible criticisms and questions. In light of this book we can see even more clearly the eminence of the Christian family and the joint mission of man and woman.

I heartily recommend the book to all who are ready to widen their perspective and pose new questions on this topic.

MIKLÓS BEER
Diocesan Bishop of Vác (Hungary)

Introduction

M Y BOOK, *The Maternal Face of God*, was published in Hungarian in 2007, and in English in 2008. As a follow-up to misunderstandings, criticisms, and reflections received since then, I would like to establish that I am not in pursuit of a new doctrine. As "one jot or one tittle shall in no wise pass away from the law" (Matt 5:18), I accept everything taught by the Catholic Church. Based on the prophetic utterance of John Paul I ("God—father, but even more mother"), more and more people have begun to accept, regarding the essence of God (*essentia divina*), that He has also a maternal face, a female side. We may also refer to Saint John Paul II's encyclical *Mulieris dignitatis*, in which he cites several passages from the Old Testament that depict God's love by "maternal" characteristics, such as this one from Isaiah: "As one whom his mother comforts, so will I comfort you" (Isaiah 66:13).[1] It is a common view among Catholics that Mary, the Mother of God, reflects for us God's maternal face in a human person. I would like to go further down this road based on perhaps only implicitly stated or divined seeds of the truth of Christian revelation (e.g., the Sophia concept) based on searching out the less-known sources of the tradition.

It should be noted here at the outset that there are a myriad of different *sophiologies* (e.g., those of Theosophy, Anthroposophy, Trinosophia), which, although referring to Jewish or Christian sources, nevertheless slide toward esotericism or New Age thinking.[2] Nevertheless, I have been wrestling with one question for years: Is it possible to establish a Christian Sophiology, a body of teaching regarding the Divine Wisdom based explicitly and emphatically on Jewish-

---

1. *Mulieris dignitatis*, 8.
2. For instance the works of Rudolf Steiner, Robert Powell, and Valentin Tomberg.

Christian revelation? This is all the more important, given that the Sophia-question is related also to that of the "female principle."

Research of the maternal side of God and the correct interpretation of Divine Wisdom may help answer and correct lopsided anthropologies (such as can be detected in feminism) and gender ideologies, which are fundamentally detrimental to sexual morality. It may also help us to recognize the true dignity of women and that of the family; moreover, it leads us to think holistically as opposed to falling into the polarizing traps of sexism and hyper-individualism. As a Greek Catholic priest and a family man, I would also like to promote the consolidation of the dignity of *marriage that is based on the love-community of man and woman.*

Following the startling title of this book I placed a question mark. The punctuation here indicates that my book deals with a hypothesis instead of a solid dogmatic statement—with a possibility, a philosophical query: *Might God be represented by a maternal face?* On what do I base such an inquiry?

I follow an interdisciplinary method. My starting point is the world of nature and man, in every aspect of which we find dichotomies, polarities, and their unity. When one seeks the roots of this phenomenon, borrowing the pattern-and-cause method of theology, one arrives at the question: Can we trace such a dichotomy in the being of the Divine? May God have a feminine side? At this point we have to recognize that in almost all great religions the Divine is represented by a feminine character as well, mainly in the form of divine wisdom and a divine marriage, the *hieros gamos,* which is the basis of all polarities and is the fundamental pattern of nuptial structures.

Wisdom (Sophia), as we shall see, almost always appears as a female character in the great religions and this prompts us to try to discover the maternal face of divinity, the feminine character of God from a Christian point of view.

I already sense an immediate criticism: this is anthropomorphism. Do we not approach God far too much with human eyes when we are looking for a feminine or maternal character in Him? But then I would ask my critics if it is anthropomorphism when Christ calls God his Father and himself the Son? Can it not be the other way around? The father, mother, and son figure of the human being is *theomorphic*: the reflection of one or another character of divine being.

Where does my concept of the maternal character of God come from? It is often believed that God is beyond any sexual determination. Others would claim that God is not simply without sex; instead, He incorporates and infinitely surpasses the characters of both sexes, by which He becomes *coincidentia oppositorum*.

I would like to pursue this train of thought from a new perspective. We may find that *Divine Wisdom*, *Sophia*, the feminine projection, the feminine face of Divine Being is present in scripture as well. It can be discovered mainly in the Old Testament, but perhaps, as we shall see, in the New Testament as well, only our preconceptions have so far made it impossible for us to see the obvious. Just as exciting should be the afterlife of this Christian principle of Sophia reviewed in mystical and modern Christian philosophers and in the liturgy and the iconography of the Church. Selected plates illustrate Sophia and related iconography in the appendix.

Besides this main line of thought, the discovery of Sophia may prove significant in addressing a number of practical questions. Furthermore, this discovery can also challenge and correct the far too patriarchal and masculine religious views that so permeate theology.

1

A World of Polarities

Polarities in Nature

RELATIONSHIP has always been a neglected category in traditional metaphysics. Among Aristotle's notions, it is an insignificant element of substances denoting physical relations only. What forms of relations can be observed in beings or in the whole of being is not an issue. Some traditional Thomists of the last century paid more attention to the specific role of relations. In Hungary, for example, Sándor Horváth wrote on the forms of relations in *Metaphysik der Relationen*, while Antal Schütz claimed that being has, beyond the *esse in* of private reality, another basic form, *esse ad*.[1]

Although Aristotelian and Thomist metaphysics do not discuss the notions of internal relations or polarities, they nevertheless deal with dichotomies or mutually interdependent effects in every aspect of existence: *dynamis* and *energeia*, that is, *potentia* and *actus* (potency and act), as well as *essentia* and *existentia* (essence and existence). Such dichotomies are valid for every finite being: the dichotomy of *hyle* and *morphe*, that is *materia* and *forma* (matter and form) for material beings (hylomorphism), and the dichotomy of *corpus* and *anima* (body and soul) for man where each pair stands in the relation of potency and action. St. Thomas Aquinas and medieval scholasticism inherited the dual vision of Aristotle's hylomorphism. Thus, as we can see, the bi-polar structure of beings is an inevitable principle even in traditional philosophies.

In observing the multi-complexity of living organisms, one

1. Antal Schütz, *Aquinói Szent Tamás szemelvényekben* [*Excerpts from St. Thomas Aquinas*] (Budapest: Szent István Társulat, 1943), 157.

notices the multiplicities of forms (*multiplicitas formarum*): whatever appears on the cellular level is bound to take shape in newer and broader units. The lower level is always in a potential state in comparison with the higher level and is delimited by a higher form (*entelechia*), by an internal program of objectives, of which the higher form, in turn, is again in a potential state for a still higher organization. As we know, Aquinas believed the highest form of man to be the intellectual *forma substantialis*: his spirit.

The dialectical systems of the modern age (Hegel and dialectical materialism) directed attention to the internal elements of existence or even of being, that were later discussed by other dialectical philosophers. However, it is obvious that so-called dialectical oppositions are not contrasts, but internal polarities present in material things. These polarities do not simply stand in opposition; they are also mutually interdependent on each other and thus represent a category in relations.[2]

The system of internal relations plays an important role in the structure of the material world. Anything that seems whole and unified from outside, this being the form of substances, within itself is characterized by complex internal relations. One may call this *internal dialectic symmetry*, whose name seems valid, since symmetry is present at all levels of organization in material things. In this light, it is important to note the hidden positive and negative elements in an atom; the competition of seed-fixing and Coulomb-forces in molecules; the dichotomies in vegetation and fauna; and the symmetry of human physiology, especially the hemispheroidal structure of the brain; the bisexual (male/female) nature of beings; and the internal duality of man, which is reflected by the opposition of body and soul. Notice that the higher we reach in the hierarchy of being, the less these oppositions appear in rigid forms, while at the level of the human being they are sublimated into love.[3]

---

2. István Cselényi, *A hit párbeszéde* [*Dialog of Faith*] (Budapest: Antikva, 1989), 35.

3. Cselényi, "Dialogical existence of man," in *Actas del IV Congreso Internacional de la S.I.T.A.*, vol. 4 (Barcelona: Società Internazionale di San Tommaso d'Aquino, 2000), 949–54.

A World of Polarities

Based on what has been said, the internal relations and polarities of things demand a new consideration in terms of ontology. Pope Benedict XVI claims that being (*Sein*) has another fundamental form besides the static, self-real form: its relational form, *esse relatum*, which he describes as waveband-like.[4] In other words, both unity and multiplicity are present in things at the same time. We are faced with a kind of relational ontology or ontological relationism that, within the analysis of being, allows a greater space to relations, to internal movements, poles, and polarities, instead of examining things from the outside. The findings of such a new ontological field may prove profitable in spheres of cosmology, biology, anthropology, and sociology as well.[5]

Relations Valid for Man

Among the possibilities of application, the sphere of personal relations requires special attention. In the discovery and re-evaluation of the category of relations, the existentialist and personalist systems that focus on personal being play a significant role.

However, before anything else, the notion of *person* requires redefinition. Boethius's idea of a person as a rational, individual substance (*substantia individua rationalis naturae*), where the most definitive category is individuality, emphasizes man's independence and his delimitation from others. A late branch of this idea is the alienation theory of existentialism (in, for example, Sartre's dictum: "*L'enfer, c'est les autres*"—Hell is other people). The personalist ideas of the twentieth century, on the other hand, ask us to recognize that we can only become persons when we open ourselves toward the other, toward other people.

Thus, at the level of personal and social being, relationship becomes a central category. A person is nothing else than the linking point of personal relationships. Everyone is surrounded by numer-

4. Joseph Ratzinger, *A keresztény hit alapjai* [*The Foundation of Christian Faith*] (Wien: Opus Mystici Corporis, 1993), 80.
5. See Cselényi, "La categoria della relazione e la comunicazione," *Aquinói Szent Tamás nyomán* (Budapest: Magyarországi Aquinói Szent Tamás Társaság, 2007), 170–81.

ous kinds of relationships. I, for example, am a priest, a teacher, a husband, a father, a driver, a consumer, a sports fan, and so forth, and each of these roles supposes a different system of relationships. A community consists of a network of relationships, and it is not a faceless mass, but the gathering of persons retaining their individuality, their multicolored plurality.

Personal relationships are much the same as polarities on the lower levels of being. The difference between the sexes, for example, is in parallel with the elements of opposing energies, with attraction and repulsion; human differences, however, are exalted into love, yearning, and gentleness. The relationship between man and woman, of course, is not only that of husband and wife, bride and bridegroom, or lovers, but also of father and daughter, mother and son.

This dichotomy of man and woman is comparable to the duality of body and soul, but the subject-object relation of the latter modifies into a subject-subject relation in the former, into intersubjectivity. This, of course, is rather an ideal condition. The roots of alienation grow out of the distortions of human relationships: the relationship between subjects descends to the level of subject-object. Such a distortion occurs when the other person is viewed as an object, like a consumer good, and not treated as a person.

Thus can the sociological content of relationships beyond the ontological be delineated. Society, therefore, is the sum of personal relationships. This, then, also means that a society can only be in balance if *personal* relationships prevail and are left free to unfold. Society has to serve human values and make way for the specific talents and values of individuals. This personalism or personalist principle is a key element in modern, democratic, and pluralist societies.

Among relationships, that of subject and object and their polarities plays a special role. It would be highly inappropriate to set off the two modes of being against one another. Object and subject, matter and spirit, body and soul are all poles or forms of a common being. Matter and body are movements in space and time, of which movement is determined by quantity; while spirit, soul, and consciousness are immaterial—divisions of space and time, that is, do not determine them; rather they are characterized by being concentrated into a single point, by self-reflection (the Thomistic *reditio completa*) that, nevertheless, will not qualify material being. And, yet, although these two forms are opposites (they stand as the most extreme polarities), they are also intimately connected.

As in human beings, body and soul can merge into the most perfect union; matter and the intellect can unify in a common reality. In man, bodily characteristics can become spiritual and spiritual characteristics bodily without the two spheres losing their own integrities. The two spheres, in spite of their opposing qualities, are mutually interdependent. Such a union becomes possible because they form two poles of a common being. Matter calls for becoming transformed into the spiritual, the intellectual into the bodily. This transformation which cannot take place in monistic systems here becomes possible because both poles are present *within* being. As Karl Rahner asserts, the body is not alien to the spirit (*Geistfremd*) and the soul is not alien to matter (*Materiefremd*); rather, both are totally open toward the other (*Geistfreund* and *Materiefreund*).

A relation between matter and the spirit is possible because a common being enfolds both the material and the spiritual being. Body and soul, matter and the spirit, the relation of object-being and subject-being are all expressions of an overarching being (the Thomistic *esse commune*) from which both sides derive. This is why it is important to work with an ontology free of extremities, to place the totality of being into the center, by the help of which we can avoid the prevailing error dominating Western thought since Descartes: the constant opposition between idealism and materialism.[6]

This is not only true within the individual existence of man, but emanates through the world as a whole. The biblical principle, according to which man's task in creation is to name things, refers to this synthesis: man humanizes the material world, endows it with intellect. On the basis of the interdependence of subject and object and their unity and openness to each other, the horizon of resurrection, where the process is complete, becomes understandable as well.

6. On the Thomistic ontology of the third millennium see Cselényi, "Risposta di San Tommaso d'Auino al problema dell'esere dell'uomo," in *Christian Humanism in the Third Millennium: The Perspective of St. Thomas Aquinas*, vol. 2 (Vatican: SITA, 2005), 246–60.

Thus relationships and their internal elements (that is, polarities), play a central role *on every level of relative being*: cosmologically in the maze of atoms and molecules; in the dichotomy of matter and form; biologically in the differences of vegetation and fauna and their complementary nature; in bisexuality and in other relations; sociologically in the world of personal bonds; anthropologically and psychologically in the relation of subject and object which is the essence of man.

Therefore, in the basic structure of being, what externally seems a unified substance and independent reality internally comprises opposing polarities and their dynamic unity. As Benedict XVI has claimed, the two most important forms of being are substance and relation, and thus the latter should be promoted among Aristotelian categories from fourth to second position.[7] This view is expressed not only theologically but also in ontological terms in the Nicaean-Constantinopolitan Creed referring to God when it declared: *moné ousia, trés hypostaseis* (one essence = one substance, three persons and the personal relations among them). Eastern theology builds its personalism on the faith of the Holy Trinity as well.[8]

And although the Eastern Church stopped short after this definition, it has tried to define the relationships among the three divine Persons more precisely. For the Eastern Church, the absolute origin is the Father: the monarchy of the Father (*moné arché* = the sole starting point or source for the other two divine Persons), from whom the Son is born and from which the Holy Spirit originates, which then, in turn, symbolize the two outreaching arms of the Father, and the work of the latter two continues in creation and leads man toward salvation (*oikonomia*). This model of the Holy Trinity then presents a starting point (*monas*)[9] within the divine essence, out of which stems a polarity (*dyas*) and the final result: the trinity (*tryas*). This is why beings created in their likeness also

---

7. Ratzinger, *Hit*, 361.

8. Cselényi, *Filozófia dióhéjban* [*Philosophy in a Nutshell*] (Esztergom: Catholic University, 2001), 35.

9. In many respects this reminds us of the Platonic/Neo-Platonic principle of *Hen* (Arch-One), out of which all other principles derive.

A World of Polarities

exhibit the characteristics of *monas, dyas,* and *tryas.* In the background of Eastern trinitology stands this sharper division between God's internal life (His *ousia*—and this, in narrow focus, is *theologia*) and His external self-expression (His *energeia*, which, in narrow focus, is *oikonomia*, leading man to salvation).[10]

It is worthwhile to clarify the theoretical basis of this distinction. As it is supposed in Eastern Christianity, God carries the duality of potential and action (*dynamis* and *energeia*). We have just referred to the aspect of energies. Western theologies find this duality impossible, primarily influenced by St. Thomas's cosmological argument based on the theory that finite beings have to be transformed from potency to act. Here, however, potency is merely a passive possibility. In the East, *dynamis* is an active potential, the divine essence. In the West this inroad is unacceptable. Western theology compiles the findings of the immanent and the salvational trinitological tenets, preferring the latter and reporting the end result only: that is, that the Holy Spirit is the sum of the work of the Father and the Son (*Filioque*).

The fact that Western trinitology explores a different route marks the richness of divine being: through different approaches the same secret can be investigated. The terms *Filioque* or *abutroque* (that the Holy Spirit is derived from both the Father *and* the Son) first establish the duality of the relationship between the Father and the Son (*dyas*); and the unity of the two is expressed in the Holy Spirit, so that an idea appears in most recent theologies that the Holy Spirit is nothing else than the relationship between the Father and the Son.[11] It is all the more apparent, then, that ancient polarities and the unity of polarities are present within divine being as well, and, accordingly, the projection of these polarities and their unity can be found in the created world.

10. Cselényi, *A hozzánk lehajló Isten* [*God Bending Down to Us*] (Nyíregyháza: Szent Athanáz Görögkatolikus Hittudományi Főiskola, 1998), 11–14. The doctrine of energies also appears in Palamite mariology.
11. Wigand Siebel, *Der heilige Geist als Relation. Eine soziale Trinitätslehre* (Münster: Herder, 1986), 41.

Western trinitology has a further implication. The tenets of the so-called psychological trinitology based on St. Augustine and St. Thomas compare the relationship of the Father and the Son to the process of cognition (*per modum cognitionis*) in which intellectual birth is described as subject and object in oppositional relation, and in which the Holy Spirit is represented by the process of love (*per modum voluntatis seu amoris*): the Spirit is the fruit of love between the Father and the Son. This trinitology, rejected by Eastern Christianity, became authoritative in the West; therefore, we have to consider its implications.

In this context, the structure of being in man is the hidden subject-object relation. That is to say that in the duality of body and soul, in the archetype of their substantial unity, and even in the source of the duality and unity of matter and the intellect, the object side cannot be termed as material at all. In conclusion, divine being is over and above both the subjectivist and the objectivist approaches and is additionally over and above the one-sided solutions of both materialism and idealism.[12] In Chapter 2, therefore, I would like to investigate how to step beyond both kinds of these half-solutions in all respects of philosophy.

In spite of all the differences just discussed, we can conclude that unity, multiplicity, and polarities have a place on every level in the structure of being.[13] The differences between Eastern and Western trinitologies show that within the broader unity of Christian beliefs various solutions and systems of co-ordinates are at work. This assumption will become meaningful in latter parts of this book.

---

12. Cselényi, *Az esse hermeneutikája* [*The Hermeneutics of esse*] (Nyíregyháza: Tudományos Testület, 2001), 104.

13. Béla Weissmahr, *Isten léte és mivolta* [*God's Existence and Essence*] (Róma: Teológiai Kiskönyvtár, 1980), 185.

2

Beyond
Materialism and Idealism

IN THIS CHAPTER I shall argue that the opposition of materialism and idealism that has prevailed in science and philosophy since Descartes is not only false, but schizophrenic. However, this opposition deserves to have its nature surveyed from the viewpoints of various branches of the sciences and of specialized philosophy.[1]

I will call the understanding of the synthesis of the two extremes *realism*. We can also call it *moderate dualism*, the *bipolar theory of being*, or *relational ontology*. This chapter, therefore, emphasizes and develops the insights of the first chapter concerning the polarity of being that characterizes all ontological strata. Let me add one remark to this: even if the idealist-subjectivist-spiritualist solution cannot be justified as one of the two poles of being, the categories of "spiritual" or "mental" can be justified. In this sense one can talk about the "moderate primacy" of the spiritual side, or, as we may call it, of the sophianic element.

Searching for Modes of
Cognition on the Level of Psychology

In this field materialism means sensualism. Its main proponents are Democritus, the British empiricists, mechanical and dialectical materialism, and positivism. The positivist Vogt, for example,

---

1. Cselényi, "Realismo di Tommaso d'Aquino e sue consequenze etiche," in *Aquinói Szent Tamás nyomán, a Magyarországi Aquinói Szent Tamás Társaság 2004-2005-ös konferenciái* (Budapest: Magyarországi Aquinói Szent Tamás Társaság, 2007), 47–68.

speaks in these terms: as urine is the product of the kidney, so thought is the product of the brain. And Lenin's definition of matter is sensualist: "All that is copied and pictured in our senses"—even though the essence of man is to transcend his senses and touch the essences.

There is, however, also an idealist extremism: innatism, a philosophy that claims that human persons possess inborn knowledge. The main proponents of this view are Plato (knowledge is only *anamnesis*, remembrance), Augustine (doctrine of illumination), Descartes (*ideae innatae*), as well as religions and philosophies that hold to the idea of reincarnation. In reality, however, we start with a *tabula rasa*.

In this context the touchstone is the realism of Aristotle and Thomas Aquinas: it proceeds from the senses, and by the help of the three levels of abstraction (sensual, mathematical, essential cognition) reaches conceptual cognition. In this sense realism is the surpassing of materialism and idealism. On the other hand, realism does not mean that it should be placed on the same level as sensual and essential cognition; we concede the primacy of intellectual cognition over these two levels.

From a logical perspective, the point of the debate of different schools is whether or not there exist universal concepts. Here the idealist solution is extreme realism (there exist only ideas—concrete things are reflections). A new formulation of this extreme realism was provided in the Middle Ages by Scotus Eriugena, and more recently by the modern pantheists.

Nominalism is another extreme (universal concepts are simply *nomen*s, names—there are only individuals). Among the philosophers and theologians upholding this view are Roscelin, William of Ockham and his followers, as well as materialists of every type.

In my view, a certain modest realism (Aristotelianism, Thomism) is the answer: universals exist and incarnate in individuals and formally in our intellect. Consequently, the solution lies between the two extremes.

From an epistemological point of view, the crux of the debate resides in questions concerning the relationship between the intellect and the external world. There has been a fourth school, skepticism, that denies the possibility of cognition. It has many types:

ancient skepticism (especially Gorgias's negation), Sophism, the *dubito ergo sum* of Descartes, Kant's criticism, Huxley's agnosticism, and the theory of the absurd found in existentialism.

The idealist (solipsist or subjectivist) solution concedes only the existence of the human intellect and the "I," whose product is the objective being, the world. Berkeley, Fichte, and Schelling are the proponents of this view; though it is not quite certain whether Schelling ever had in mind a single "I."

The materialist solution is that matter defines mind. In truth, however, the human mind can actively form the external world.

The answer to materialism is epistemological realism: the human mind has no creative power; rather is there an interplay of mind and being, since the objective world is not identical with matter. The modest primacy of the spiritual side can be argued, therefore, since the mind is not only a reflection but is able to form the world.

Anthropologically, then, we are interested in the constituent parts of man, their quantity and inner relation, two variations of which are trichotomy (body-mind-spirit) and dichotomy (body-mind). In addition, there exist many types of parallelism (such as that of Descartes, of Spinoza, or of Jung), but these do not provide a sure path to the problem's resolution. On the one hand, the idealist solution is to offer a sharp dualism, where there is only one single substance, spirit. According to this view, the body is only an illusion (viz. Pythagoreanism and Platonism; this is the fundamental principal of the doctrine of the immortality of the soul). Manichaeism can also be listed here; it concedes the material and spiritual constituent parts, but despises the body in favor of the glorification of the soul. There is another solution, however, which is to argue that the soul is not a substance, but only a process. There is no charioteer, so to speak, only a chariot. This is precisely the foundation of the Hindu doctrine of reincarnation, i.e., the claim that there is no personal immortality.

Turning to the materialist solution, it appears that there is only one substance: the body (or, in other words, the brain), which possesses mind as an accident. Modest dualism or realism (and relational ontology) says that the body exists as well as the soul. Both are *substantia incompleta*, that is, incomplete substances, and the two form a unity of being, wherein the soul is *forma substantialis*, the essence-providing, forming, entelechy, program of human being. At this point we transcend the incomplete solutions of idealism and materialism, and we clearly see that, in comparison to the body, the intellectual-spiritual capacity is the active and form-providing part of the human being.

One can observe the same phenomenon on the ethical level. Hedonism, utilitarianism, and consumerism result from materialism; applied materialism, however, results from a one-sided view of man.

Sharp dualism and its rejection of the body result from idealism, as for example in Gnosticism, Neoplatonism, and religions of the Far East. Relativism or negation of the fundamental order results from subjectivism and, as a consequence, nihilism manifests in existentialism.

The synthesis of sharp dualism coincides with the realist approach: we have brought to perfection all the capacities of our soul, body, and the unity of our personality. In this context, this synthesis means a harmony of the material and the subjective order. The primary of the two, however, is the spiritual.

Sociologically, collectivism follows from materialism, which leads to the decline of the human person. On the other hand, individualism, that is capitalism and neoliberalism, follows from subjectivism.

Realism leads to personalism, wherein persons as well as the community will never be distorted. This is why Jacques Maritain stresses the *primauté de spirituel*, the primacy of the spiritual, in his personalism. There is only one way to become a person in the full sense of the word: by experiencing one's own soul.

In metaphysics we usually project the body-mind duality onto the realm of entities. From Descartes comes the classical formulation of dualism: *res cogitans* and *res extensa*, which is actually the duality of spirit and matter. According to this view, there are only two worldviews: the materialist and the idealist (or spiritualist). The most important figures of materialism are the British empiricists, mechanical (Holbach, La Mettrie) and dialectical materialists, and the positivists, whereas the major idealists include Berkeley, Fichte, and Schelling. Sartre belongs to a separate category; since he identi-

fies being with matter, he emphasizes the experienced human existence and so follows the pathway of subjective idealism.

Now, my claim is that there is a separate world in us, which exists
exclusively in us. This, however, is the level only of a spiritual phenomenon that has no creative power. There is only a certain transfiguration, a transition between the two sides:

> The body becomes soul,
> Objects start to fly
> On the shoulder of the thought,
> The stone stands on his feet,
> Dances like a lively woman…
> Weight is weightless,
> Object is a subject:
> Transforms everything into its opposite
> Under the sun:
> Only you see this miraculous
> Metamorphosis of being.

Finally, we have to concede the mutually penetrating unity of
matter and spirit, and of body and soul. This is how realism understands it. Nevertheless, we can also see that there is no identity or
equality, but only the primacy of the intellectual-spiritual. However,
in ontology, the theory of being, we deploy metaphysical concepts
in a wider sense.

Materialism, first of all, reduces being to matter. Idealism, on the
other hand, reduces being to mind. Both are reductionist strategies,
whereas the solution lies in claiming the double-faced nature of
being. There is something tremendously important in the teachings
of St. Thomas, who says that being (as *perfectio perfectionum*) is
beyond the extremes of object and subject, since it comprises both.
As Karl Rahner asserts, the body is not alien to the intellect and the
soul is not alien to matter. Rather, both are totally open toward the
other; they are "friends." In other words, their relationship is man-
woman-dual-unity-like, that is, being has a nuptial character.

Theologically the same applies to the Absolute. Materialist theology is in itself a contradiction, though there are different forms
of idealist monism, such as in Platonism, religions of the East, as
well as in the modern pantheism of Spinoza and Leibniz, in Hegel's

idealism, and in the cosmic monism of the so-called "New Age." Independently of whether we investigate the materialist or the idealist versions of monism, both have a deficiency: the paradox of the developing Absolute (since it is an absolute, it may not change, develop). As a consequence both materialists and idealists confuse the notions of the absolute and the relative. I also reject the Hindu solution of saying that *Atman* is part of *Brahman* or else it doesn't have real existence.

The solution of objective idealism might be a good one. Objective idealism says that the leading principle of the world is the divine mind. It can be found in numerous readings from Classical Greek thought (*nous, logos, pneuma,* and *psyche* govern the world) as well as in the Jewish-Christian doctrine of creation. One can find the same idea in the arguments for the existence of God, i.e., that divine thought can be found in everything. Nonetheless, it is not merely idealism, since things are not only ideas, but possess real existence.

Realism is, therefore, the only solution: reality, being (*esse commune*) is beyond all materialist and idealist monisms; there is no tension between matter and spirit, but interdependence, being is as a matter of fact double-faced. God, who—as St. Thomas says—is *esse ipsum,* being in itself, immensely transcends both forms of existence.[2] On the other hand, both have their origin in him, in as much as the conscious, spiritual part is primary, and whereby man—by his spirituality—has been created in the likeness of God, who is "spirit" (John 4:24). Moreover, taking into consideration the main points of the psychological Trinity, we can say that God comprises the objective and subjective life as well as the unity of the two, which is reflected in the duality of the matter and mind on the level of created life as well as in the unity of the two.

To summarize our journey so far: there is complementarity between matter and spirit:

> *Two infinites:*
> *the outside and the inside*
> *we carry the other from the beginning*

2. "*Perfectio omnium perfectionum*" (perfection of all perfections), *De potentia* q. 7, a. 2 ad 9.

the bearing of our nuptials
a growing world.

The struggle of matter and spirit is not a "game ended in a draw," so to speak. Nor is it a wrestling, nor a simple antithesis. It is an interdependence: one has to observe them from the viewpoint of a higher perspective of unity. As Aquinas marvelously expresses it: *"cum suum esse sit suum intelligere."*[3] This is to say that objective and subjective being form one unit as, according to Aristotle, truth is the correspondence of being and intellect.[4]

This theory again justifies the primacy of the conscious being, of the spiritual,[5] since, in accordance with what we have said above, the total apprehension of being is the apprehension of being interwoven by intellect. This dominance justifies the comprehensive primacy of the principal order, thought, intellect, and (as we will call it) the principle of Sophia in contrast to the bodily side within the totality of being. Within the divine being, the Father-Son relationship reminds us of the bipolarity of objective and subjective being, whereas, according to the accepted Western view, their unity is represented by the Holy Spirit. Since, as we have seen so far, there is a certain plurality in the understanding of the divine existence, we cannot exclude other solutions. Let me explain it in a few words: the crux of the problem is the duality of the Father and the Holy Spirit and the fruit of their unity of being, the Son, wherein the Holy Spirit is the vehicle of the theory of Sophia and the leading principle of the reasonable order of the world.

3. S. Th. I. q. 14, a. 5.
4. "Adaequatio rei et intellectus."
5. N.B.: We are talking about primacy here, not its singular nature and by no means about the nothingness of the other!

3

The Nuptial
Structure of Being

HOPEFULLY, I have managed to demonstrate thus far that we meet polarities in every field of being. In this chapter I would like to show that this polar structure leads to the family structure of being and to the recognition of its nuptial ontology. In other words, dualities and unities at a human level are similar to both the husband-wife and the child-parent relationships and point toward them.[1] But let us change our line of investigation and proceed not from bottom to top, or from top to bottom, but rather from the middle, from the sphere of the human phenomenon, and let us try to extrapolate the experience we gain here and apply it to nature.

The unity and duality of man and woman is one of the building blocks of our life. In what follows I am going to unfold the threads of this experience in the sphere of the universal. I would like to explore how this unity/duality manifests itself as a phenomenon, and how deeply it is rooted in being from an ontological point of view.[2]

Man and Woman as "Phenomena"

The differences (and the attraction) between man and woman are among the most colorful, exciting, and tender characteristics of human beings. They have been the source of paternal and maternal

---

1. Cselényi, *Családegyház* [*Family-Church*] (Esztergom: Rác-templom Alapítvány, 2001), 38.
2. Cselényi, *Hit*, 130.

feelings, a child's love for its parents, fleeting and eternal love, fidelity and infidelity, passion and transfiguration, ecstasy and agony, worry and jealousy, affection and hatred, nobility and dehumanization, virtue and sin, peace and struggle throughout history. They have been a source of inspiration in art and poetry and the driving force behind the development of mankind. They are a complex, intricate reality.

First of all, we should have a look at the relationship between man and woman from a biological point of view. That is where the differences are most apparent. Beyond the common, universal constitution of the human body, sexual characteristics are a source of basic physiological differences. Sexuality, the roots of which reach back to prehistoric times, to the animal world, is one of the strongest drives. In the case of humans, the preservation of the species is not sex's only purpose. Indeed, it has an effect on every phase of our lives. It transforms children into young men and women during puberty; it determines many of our characteristics in adulthood; it contributes to our happiness in a number of ways; and it accompanies us throughout the years of change all the way to old age.

In a way, the sexuality of man and woman is different, and in another way these differences complement each other. The contrast is not always obvious. There are special cases when overlaps and dualities appear (bisexuality, problems in sexual life). But, for most of the population, there is a clear line between the two genders. Men usually have a stronger physique than women. The biological constitution of women points toward motherhood.

The mutuality of the two sexes is just as apparent. They complement each other, which is manifested not only in sexual life, but in almost every field of existence. According to statistics, the number of men and women remains nearly equal. This balance could provide a natural basis for married life if it were not upset by wars from time to time.

The disparity and unity between man and woman is not only a physiological, but is at least as much a psychological fact. Undoubtedly, there are even more differences in this field, though it is not always easy to distinguish purely "masculine" and "feminine" characteristics from each other. According to psychologists, the personality traits of the opposite sex are latent in each individual. In everyday life we can find several examples for the above from the "henpecked husband" to the "shrewish woman." Besides a number of other factors, it is the proportion of the two orientations in sexuality that determines the personality of an individual.

C.G. Jung holds that there is a male soul, the *animus*, and a female soul, the *anima*. Both men and women possess the characteristics of their partner and form a reality together. According to Jung, men tend to be extroverts; their function is the formation of objects and things. Women, on the other hand, tend to be introverts, interested mainly in internal values. Jung describes men with the word *Haben* (possession), and women with the word *Sein* (being, life).[3]

Today, the social roles of men and women are changing as they assume new responsibilities at home and in the workplace. However, if we want to assess the current situation, we should beware of two extremes. One extreme would be to declare the family and social structures of olden days as universal. We should support women's rights movements in order to help women assume roles that they were not allowed to before. But we should avoid the other extreme: no equal rights movement should have a goal to feminize men or make women more masculine. Our roles in life might change, but neither sex should give up its basic characteristics and its unique values, which are the product of physiological and social conditions. On the contrary, we should preserve these values. Women should preserve their most natural role, that of motherhood; and they should likewise preserve their receptiveness, their thoughtfulness, and their sense of beauty. They can only gain from these characteristics in their role; they cannot lose through them. And men do not violate the equal rights of women either by providing support and security for the family or by working hard and performing well in their profession.

---

3. N.B.: Genesis calls Eve the mother of life (*Hávah*) from the word: *hájáh* = life, being.

The Maternal Face of God?

The Roots of the Unity of Man and Woman

The duality and unity of man and woman point beyond the simple "facts." Rather, the duality and unity of man and woman have the force of revelation. They reveal all those differences and the unity resulting from these differences which can be found everywhere.

The direct root of psychological differences lies in our different roles in society. These roles, however, are based on biological foundations. Sexual polarity is a higher manifestation of the polarity of life and matter (for example positive and negative charge). The human being and the relationship between man and woman is the product of this ontological background.

The world is a developing, moving reality. A number of people have tried to describe the essence of its movement with simple formulae. Democritus, for instance, described it as the unification and separation of particles. Neoplatonists have described it as a struggle between matter and spirit. Aristotle saw the duality of matter and form in things. We should observe that in most languages the term *matter* is derived from the word *mother* (*materia* from *mater*); therefore, it represents the maternal, feminine side of things. On the other hand, *form* represents *actus*; it is the active, "masculine" side of things. The other word pairs of Aristotle (potency-act, essence-existence, body-soul) also include two sides (feminine and masculine). The dualisms and parallelisms of later ages all assume the existence of these two sides.

We should pay attention to the fact that in most languages, especially in the Indo-European languages, a system has been developed for the grammatical gender of words. An analysis of that system would go beyond the scope of the present study, but we should state one principle: since language (according to Heidegger) is a declaration concerning being, masculine or feminine nouns are the representation of the duality and bisexuality of being. They are indicative of, that is, the nuptial structure of being. To mention another example: *potentia* is a feminine and *actus* a masculine word. They show that everything has a receiving, feminine side as well as an active, forming side; the two together constitute reality. The old masters knew very well why they treated a concept as masculine, feminine, and the balance of the two: neuter. All that is the representation of ancient wisdom.

Furthermore, let us say extrapolation on a cosmic scope is also possible. It may seem like a simplification, but there are two forces present in everything. One is disintegration, the other is unification. The universe is expanding, but at the same time in certain places matter becomes concentrated and organized, resulting in such developments as the birth of mankind. Teilhard de Chardin sees these two tendencies in the duality of radial and tangential energy, which he calls the *Eternal Masculine* and *Eternal Feminine*.[4] (Later on we will return to this question.)

We may be right in believing that, due to psychological traits, the duality of man and woman is a representation of the same polarity at a higher level that characterizes matter, too. Therefore, man really is a "microcosm," a small world that experiences the "problems" and internal tendencies of the entire universe.[5] Man with his energies directed outwards (extrovert) represents the propagation of created being, while woman is the collecting, unifying concept (introvert) holding together the creation of man and making his life more stable. This is the cosmic root of love and the unity of man and woman.

One way of putting it is to say that *love may be found in matter*, that is, love is the higher representation of a unity born out of duality (dialectics, polar structure), which is already present in matter. That is how we can understand the real meaning of the community of man and woman and the meaning of marriage and family. The relationship between the two sexes reminds us of the contrast and unity of potency and act, essence and existence, matter and form, body and soul, matter and consciousness. It is the highest representation of the polarities in the created world. In this duality, women represent emotional receptiveness, intimacy, and a desire for completeness, and men represent power and dynamism. Therefore, sexuality, love, and marriage go beyond the boundaries of biology. Being does not only consist of polarities, but (with an analogous

---

4. Pierre Teilhard de Chardin, *Le féminin ou l'unitif* (Paris: Cerf, 1965), 78.

5. Emile Rideau, "La sexualité," in *Nouvelle Revue théologique* 58 (Paris: Cerf, 1968), 180.

word) it has a nuptial structure; it reveals solutions similar to the duality and unity of man and woman in every sphere.

For the sake of the main topic of my thesis—the Sophia theory—we should define more clearly the analogy of metaphysical-ontological word pairs and sexuality. It is not immediately apparent which is the "feminine" and which is the "masculine" side of a "pair." The "place" of potency and act is quite clear. In essence and existence, *essentia* (*idea, entelecheia*) is the feminine, maternal component. Although existence is a feminine word, Aquinas puts it more clearly: this is *actus existendi*, the existential order, the activating masculine component; for it is existence that makes real the possibility of an essence.[6] According to the greatest metaphysical schools, essential order is linked to what gives meaning: wisdom. Therefore, as we will see, essence is rightly connected to the Sophia theory.[7]

The relationship between matter and form, body and soul, is not immediately apparent. Matter, as we have seen, is a maternal element. However, grammatically, *morphe* (form) or soul (*anima*, or *Seele* in German) are feminine words, and these concepts are on the side of act. There are three possible ways to resolve this contradiction:

1. For Aristotle and Aquinas, matter (*hyle* or *materia*) is not a secondary substance, equipped with secondary features. Rather, it is primary matter (*materia prima*) that does not yet exist; it is only a possibility. Today by matter we mean a specific, visible material, which is the "external shell" of things. The ancients described this as a phenomenon (*phainomenon*) and believed that it was determined by the internal divine core (*noumenon*), essence (*ousia*), invisible form. The relationship between body and soul can be seen as a relationship in which the soul is the determining factor. The body, in this way of thinking, is only an external shell, a type of clothing, a secondary system. In sophiological literature, which deals with the question of *hokmah* (= sophia) in scripture, we will meet the following approach: the body is only a type of clothing, an external shell covering the meaningful essence.

6. Aquinas: "Something exists only insofar as it participates in being." In *evang. Joan.*, Prol., n. 5.
7. For example the pattern of *rationes seminales* mentioned by Augustine.

2. Even if we insist on a literal hylemorphism, it is still true that form is an act compared to the possibility of matter, or *materia prima*. But by creating the internal core of existing matter as *forma substantialis* it only creates the *essence* (idea, meaningful internal content) of existing matter, which is only a potential itself. It still has to be activated. It is the feminine, maternal element in the creation of existing matter, which will have to be actualized by the act of existence (*actus existendi* being the "masculine" element). We could put it this way: essential order (*ordo essentialis*) is the maternal side of created things, while existing order (*ordo existentialis*) is the masculine side. Matter is the unity of both.

3. Matter is actualized by form and the body is actualized by the soul (in both cases of the *materia prima* and *materia secunda*). However, as Jung points out, the soul itself has two sides: *anima* and *animus*, which are polarized and join each other in a nuptial structure. Therefore, the form, the soul, and the intellectual each have a "feminine" and a "masculine" side as well.

But we can even go beyond this point. In a later chapter we will see that the theme of a *World-Soul* (mostly seen as feminine and maternal) also appears at a cosmic level, which—based on Christian principles—is often associated with the *Logos* as the "bridegroom" pair of a World-Soul/mother-bride within the framework of a kind of "*hieros gamos*."

In conclusion, if the duality of man and woman (the nuptial structure) is so much part of the structure of being from individual beings to the entire universe, then it might be fairly safe to say that this duality and unity are (metaphorically) also *present in divine being*. In other words, the divine being has not only a masculine, but perhaps a feminine, maternal side, as well. But an elaborate interpretation of the above requires further research and enquiry.

4

The Principle of Sophia
in Hellenic Philosophy

Ascertainments so far:
1. Being has a polar structure.
2. Everything has (analogically) a masculine and a feminine side.
3. Among the polarities of body and soul, external and internal, the polarity spiritual-intellectual enjoys priority.
4. The forming principle of things and the world is an intelligent, organizing principle.
5. This principle is the principle of wisdom, Sophia.

Verbal Forms of the Principle of Wisdom

IN THIS CHAPTER we will examine the verbal forms and philosophical expressions of the principle of wisdom in classical Greek philosophy. Eight different terms are relevant: *logos, idea, nous, demiourgos, eikon, pneuma, psyche,* and *sophia.* The clarification of these terms is necessary before continuing our investigation.[1]

1. The term *logos* derives from the Greek word *legein* (to say), the Latin variation of which is *legere* meaning to read, to count, to speak. A further etymological change has modified it to mean *word* or *speech.* In another context, it can refer to the sense or meaning of something or someone that stands behind the word, the intellect that has the ability to think and to speak. This is how we reach the human or divine intellect, the creator. On the other hand, the ratio-

---

1. Thomas Schipflinger, *Sophia-Maria: Eine Ganzheitliche Vision der Schöpfung* (München-Zürich: Neue Stadt, 1988), 231.

nal ability of an intelligent being leads us to ideas, our next term. *Logos* is the carrier of ideas and the ultimate result is the World-Spirit, World-Intellect, or World-Soul.

2. The term *idea* derives from the root *id-vid* (viz. the Latin term *videre*): to look in general or to look *at* something which, in turn, means to grasp the essence of things. Objects are the realizations of their ideas insofar as the idea descends into the material as the embodiment of notions. The descending notion has been termed *logos noetos*, the materialized idea *logos aesthetos*. In this sense the terms *logos* and *idea* saturate each other. The Greek term *noetos* (*noein* = to think, viz. *Nous*) marks notions that can be comprehended by thinking, while the term *aesthetos* (*aisthanesthai* = to comprehend with the senses, viz. aesthetics) marks notions that are visible, perceivable. Thus the terms *logos* and *nous* also saturate each other.

3. The term *nous*, as we have seen, derives from *noein* (to think, to understand), and as such it is synonymous with the ultimate meaning of *logos*. However, both *logos* and *nous* allude to *idea idearum*, the foundation and overall content of individual ideas and essences. According to some philosophers *nous* is also a synonym of *demiourgos*.

4. The term *demiourgos* derives from *demos* (people) and *ergo* (to do, to create) and thus it is a creator, a builder, an artist, a being who shapes the world.

5. The term *eikon* derives from *eiken* (to mirror) and thus it is a picture, an image, a reflection, an icon.

6. The term *pneuma* derives from *pneuso* (to blow, to breathe, to live) just as the Latin term *spiritus* derives from *spirare* (to breathe) and both mark in man the airy, immaterial element, his spirit.

7. The term *psyche* derives from *psychein* (to cool, to enliven, to animate) and thus it is breath, spirit, soul, vitality, heart, aptitude, emotion, courage, inclination.

8. The term *sophia* derives from the adjective *sophos* (wise, clever, intelligent, cunning, smart) and thus it signifies wisdom, cleverness, slyness, and artistic ability. For some philosophers its synonym is *pneuma*, for others *psyche*. The Latin term for sophia, *sapientia*, derives from *sapere* (to know, to feel).

The Principle of Sophia in Hellenic Philosophy

After considering the various terms, *logos, nous, demiourgos, pneuma*, and *psyche* seem to signify an intelligent, creative subject, a person, a rational being, a rational substance, whereas *sophia* signifies a rational ability (yet it can be an active subject and a rational process as well) and *logos, idea,* and *eikon* the consequences of the rational act. The pairs or polarities can also be identified according to their genders: *logos, nous,* and *demiourgos* are active and masculine, whereas *sophia (sapientia), psyche,* and *idea* are receptive and feminine. In between, perhaps because they bear characteristics of both sides, stand the neuter-gendered *pneuma* and *eikon*.[2]

From the point of view of our investigation, *sophia* is the most important term. In ancient Greece the term *sophia* originally had been used in an ethical and craftsman-like context and only gained philosophical meanings later in the form of World-Soul where it is the organizing principle of the world, its rationalizing element: *idea idearum* (viz. what had been said of the primacy of the spiritual-intellectual) as *demiourgos* and his counterpart are in creation (viz. what had been said of the nuptial structure of being), and perhaps just because of this it can be a substitute for one or another meaning of *logos* or *nous*.

Thomas Schipflinger,[3] who has done much to encourage the acceptance of sophiology in the Catholic Church, points out that a synonym of *sophia*, the most important notion in Plato, is *kalon* (nice, good, noble, precious, and happy). *Kalon*, on the other hand, has the same root as *holon* (whole, complete, healthy), out of which the word "catholic" derives (*kat'holon* = according to the whole, entire, universal) along with terms like "holistic," the Old German *Hail* and Modern German *Heil* (salvation and *heilig* = sacred, holy) or the English word "whole."

Thus the term *sophia* with all its connotations, allusions, and associations draws one's attention to see things in their totality, to

---

2. Similar pairs of terms appear in the Old Testament: *davar* (= verb, the Word of God) and *ruah* (= spirit, the spirit of God), and even in Islam: *kalam* (= speech, the will of God) and *ruh* (= spirit, the spirit of God), which all represent masculine and feminine genders respectively.

3. A professor of the Jesuit order, conducting research on the history of religion at the *Ostkirchliches Institut* in Regensburg, Germany.

discover relations (viz. *intellectus* and *inter-legere* = to read between the lines), to think globally, holistically, to seek totality, to be healthy or "whole" in body and soul. It also encourages us toward salvation and happiness, and not so much to rationality and analysis, but, rather, it merges the analytical with the practical, the intentional with the emotional, and expresses a unifying world picture.

The Intellect Shaping the
World in Ancient Greek Culture

Before systematic philosophy, the idea that the Earth or the entire world is held together, governed, and animated by a divine power had been present in myth. This ability was bestowed on a goddess in Greek mythology, Gaia, the goddess of the Earth (named Gaea, Terra, or Tellus by the Romans). According to Hesiod, Gaia was created out of chaos. She was given life by Uranus, the god of the sky, without female assistance, who then wedded her and out of their relation the Titans came to be born. Gaia's temple was in Delphi and she was the goddess creator of all life on Earth. Similar motifs appear in all cultures. Myth and natural religion considered the world animate and the parallel of the micro- and the macrocosms they recognized as reality.[4]

Philosophy followed myth. Classical Greek thought looked for an ultimate explanation, the *arche*, and set the goal to find *sophia* or wisdom. Pythagoras (624–545 BC) coined the name *philo-sophia* (aiming at wisdom) in which *philein* means to love, to prefer, to strive for. And although the Greeks believed the material world eternal, from the beginning they were convinced that its ornamented face was created by a divine organizing power or intellect.[5] Hellenic philosophers, however, did not clarify the ontological aspects of this principle, failing to differentiate between the absolute and the relative levels of being. Thus an array of pantheist colors were ascribed to the divine Intellect.

4. Bargatsky, *Universum*, 85.
5. Cselényi, *Filozófia*, 11.

The Principle of Sophia in Hellenic Philosophy

The idea of *logos* first appeared in Heraclitus around 500 BC for whom it meant a wise and universal Intellect which unites opposites within itself and which provides sense to everything but which man cannot understand. For the atomist philosopher Anaxagoras the same idea is *nous*. The dialectical element already present in Heraclitus is furthered by Empedocles: things are driven by the opposites of *philetos* (love) and *neicos* (discord).

In Plato (427–347 BC), *logos* gains a logical character; for him the Heraclitean *logos* is replaced by *nous* and *idea*. Plato's starting point is *nous*, the idea of ideas from which all subsequent ideas originate, and his own primary principles are lowered to the level of matter that is shaped into Cosmos by the world-forming *Demiourgos* (*nous*) out of eternal substances. Thereafter a world-spirit (*psyche*, *pneuma*, *sophia*, *the idea of ideas*) shapes individual beings out of these substances with *pronoia* (care, prudence, wisdom, force). Thus the world, the cosmos, is the materialized idea of ideas, the universal animal whose body is the world of matter and whose soul is the universal spirit, *nous*. The world is fine and benevolent just as in the Christian belief of creation.[6]

Plato was the first philosopher who considered the cosmos a single living creature animated by the universal spirit. In the *Timaeus* he claims: "God created the single Whole out of independent particles as a perfect living creature untouched by time and disease.... He compiled the universe as he provided intellect to man's spirit and spirit to his body, so that his work would be complete in superior and natural beauty and ingenuity. This is why we can declare that our universe is a spiritual and effectively intellectual being."[7]

According to Plato's disciple, Aristotle (384–322 BC), an internally programmed aim, *entelecheia* (*en* = in, *telos* = aim, goal) is present in every single individual. In his famous sky-model, the spheres circle in the shape of transparent crystal globes around the Unmoved Mover (*Kinesis akineton*) who operates as a Universal Spirit. This

---

6. Viz. the goodness of the world declared by God in Genesis at the end of each day.

7. Cited by Walter Bargatsky, *Das Universum lebt: Die aufsehenerregende Hypothèse vom organischen Aufbau des Weltall* (München: Heine, 1978), 26.

concept dominated philosophy and theology throughout the Middle Ages, but for Aristotle the spheres were still living creatures who are guided by their internal spirit or *entelecheia*.

Heraclitus's idea of *logos* reappears around 300 BC in Stoic philosophy. Cosmos is a material reality energized by an inherently universal *logos* whose various effects are termed in a number of ways. It is *fatum* in so far as it determines the movement of matter in space. It is *nomos* when it structuralizes (viz. the laws of nature), and *pneuma* when it animates matter. The symbol of *pneuma* is fire: a dynamic intellectual force.[8] Furthermore, it is *pneuma* that keeps the various forms of being alive; it is a kind of maxim in inorganic and especially organic beings, soul in animals, intellect in man, and World-Soul in the universe. This World-Soul, however, does not only animate things, but it also descends into the universe to become *pronoia* (a caretaker spirit); its elements are found in everything as *logoi spermatikoi* (intellectual seeds) and *ratio seminalis*, which are already present in *logos*, but have descended into things.

Pneuma is a fine, ethereal, spiritual, effectively fiery force (*pyr technikon*) whose highest form is the *pronoia-World-Soul* from one point of view, being equivalent with the universal and immanent *logos*, but, from another perspective, it can be considered as an independent mediator. Individual beings, including man, merge through *pronoia* into family-like unions. This cosmopolitan relation is *sympathyia* (an existential, physical, unique reality) and we experience this *sympatheia* in the sense of all beings having been joined into one.

Thus far we have treated *logos kosmikos*. Yet Stoic philosophy also considered the term *logos orthos* (the true Logos) and believed it utterly important: they recognized the various aspects of *logos kosmikos* (*fatum*, *nomos*, *pneuma*) and experienced it in appropriate speech and lifestyle. A wise man, that is, knows *logos*, experiences it in *sympathyia* and *sympatheia* and, as a result, his serenity is imperturbable. This is where Stoic serenity and resignation come from. Such a view nowadays could be considered as an organic religion

8. Another interesting parallel: Symbols of the Holy Spirit in *The New Testament* include fire, whirlwind, and spring of water.

and categorized as a world-immanent, pantheist monism. Regardless, Stoicism, as the most prominent philosophy of Hellenism, had a great effect on authors of the New Testament, especially St. John, who uses the terms *Logos* and *Pneuma* (*Word* and *Spirit*)[9] for two of the transcendent Persons of the Holy Trinity.

The dual term of *nous-pneuma* appears as *nous-psyche* in another branch of Hellenism, Neoplatonism. Plotinus does not recognize the world as having been created; he extrapolates a theory of emanation: the world emanates from *Hen* (the One), is formed by *nous*, and then by *psyche*. Regardless whether we consider the dichotomies of *logos-pneuma*, *nous-psyche*, *demiourgos-sophia*, or even *philotes* and *neikos*, all pairs are married in the principle of man and woman and form a sacred union, a *hieros gamos* playing on the robustly active and aesthetically receptive sides of divine being.

Neoplatonic philosophy inherited the idea of an animate cosmos from the Stoics, and their influence can be traced to the late Middle Ages. Plotinus expresses his esteem for the world against what he took to be the position of Christian thinkers: "Man is unable to worship invisible gods if he overemphasizes their visible image. How can it be that some of the vilest men are considered immortal while heaven and the stars are denied a spirit? The order and beauty of the universe, once we see it as physical reality, shows that its spirit must be superior to man's spirit."[10]

The overall teaching of ancient Greek wisdom on the world-forming Divine Intellect has had far-reaching effects. It influenced the Old Testament (viz. the literature of wisdom) and Christian thought through the mediation of Philo[11] and then directly through St. Clement of Alexandria, Origen, and St. Augustine, and can be caught specifically in such terms as *rationes seminales* (in St. Augustine), natural law, cardinal virtues, responsibility, conscience, and natural right.

9. Cselényi, *Filozófia*, 16.

10. Bargatsky, *Universum*, 29.

11. Philo could be treated here with Neoplatonists, but we will discuss his ideas when we elaborate on the notion of Sophia in the Old Testament.

However, and this is important from our present perspective, many voices of ancient Greek philosophy are echoed in later modifications of the wisdom-principle and the dichotomy of *Logos-Sophia*,[12] which indicates not only a servile adaptation of the ideas, but their reconceptualization, as well as embedding the truths of revelation. The authors of the Bible, that is, trim the Greek notions of their pantheist and polytheist overtones, but, as we shall see, a number of motifs found a place in the transcendent idea of God also.

Logos and Sophia in Gnosticism

The pair of terms, Logos and Sophia, already appeared in the literature of Gnosticism that had aligned itself to some degree with Greek thought; in many respects it was its complement and its rival as it was also a rival of early Christianity. Naturally, we only touch on this broad area of philosophy from the perspective of our present investigation.

It is customary to delineate three strands of Gnosticism: the Egyptian, the Persian-Manichean, and the Greek-Hellenic. The most renowned is the Manichean with its sharp dualism. However, a fourth ancient strand is hidden among the three, the Mandaean. Mandaean sources reveal a monistic view, whereas in Manicheanism a quasi-dualism appears, while in the Hellenic strand, perhaps as an influence of Plato and Neoplatonism, we find a rigid dualism, especially in Marcion, where the king of darkness is identified with the material world and has no pre-cosmic being, but, rather, is an anti-divine force at war with the realm of the Light-Father.[13]

The starting point of Mandaean Gnosticism is Logos. The first aspect of the Gnostic Logos is life. Life stands above all else, and out of which the first, the second, and all subsequent lives derive. This life in its essence is alien in our world because it arrives from another, hidden, unknown, and secretive being. Generally, this alien life appears as *Father* in Gnosticism, while in the Neoplatonic variety we see it as a world beyond all else.

---

12. Schipflinger, *Sophia*, 39.
13. Róbert Csank, *A gnoszticizmus* [*Gnosticism*] (Debrecen: 2003).

The Principle of Sophia in Hellenic Philosophy

What we see here is crystal-clear monism; there are no two gods present, one wicked, one benevolent, no duality of matter and spirit. But Logos presents itself by descending into the world in a quasi-dualism as a result of the splitting and transformation of Light, at the end of which process stands man. The entire process arrives in polytheism with its internal content retaining its monotheist character all along the way. Everything and everyone is solely the transfiguration and imagination of Logos.

In Gnosticism, life has changed its abode in the world-beyond for a worldly space, but since to live in this world (because of the unknown) carries dangers, the world, from a favorable perspective, gains the meaning of a shelter that protects its inhabitants and prevents their falling apart. From both a cosmogonic and an anthropogenic aspect, both the universe and the body can be seen as a shelter. The body, from still another point of view, is a tent, garment, or temple, all which symbolically can refer to the world-at-large.

Here we arrive at a point of primary importance in the discussion of the Gnostic worldview. The dismissal and the hatred of matter, of the body, and of the world on behalf of Gnostic schools or other extremely ascetic related groups is well known. This, in part, might be accepted, if we consider that the clothing of life, according to Gnosticism, was light in the world-beyond, which it had received from the first life and which thus originally was absolutely free. However, the world is judged evil, a cause of suffering, and a counterforce of light in Gnostic mythology only from this extreme, absolutist, and eschatological aspect.

Although living in this world is burdened with suffering, compared to relegations and degradations later to come, our world is still a protective shelter and, as everyone's home, is instrumental in guarding life. It is a shelter and a place to gather strength, a place to gather the powers falling apart from within ourselves until life can step safely onto a higher level. The paradox of the Gnostic Logos revolves around its view of the materialized world as a counterforce; whereas it accepts its own time and spatiality, it also respects its new and alien home, and respects the adversary that holds it prisoner: the light of Gnosticism contemplates the darkness of the world with interest, strains to know it better so that once in the future it can defeat it. As a matter of fact, this is where the cosmological drama of Gnosticism begins, in which drama the forces and counter-forces present in Logos duel. Gnosticism experiences genesis as the primary fall.

At this point, one notices a definite difference between Judeo-Christianity and Gnosticism. Whereas in Genesis, God comprehends the creation of the world and man as a positive act—and man only becomes degraded after his fall—in the Gnostic concept of creation, life (light) falls into the darkness of the world, and it is a tragedy for the spirit born out of Life to be placed into a body and to awaken as man.

Gnostic schools provide various explanations as to the reason of the primary fall where the freedom of the Absolute is restricted: "Who has imprisoned me as I set forth from my home, from my parents who had brought me up?"[14] The motif of being imprisoned is a recurring theme in Manichean texts as well, where the synonyms of body are such terms as "prison," "net," and "snare."[15] The freedom of Life becomes an alien fate as if an external power would force its descent and subsequent fall. (This train of thought, obviously, strongly leans toward dualism.)

Greek Gnosticism, especially in Plotinus, provides a different answer. The primary spirit separated from the world beyond turns away from its creator, and out of curiosity[16] strives for the unknown (primary fall), bending toward something unnoticed lower in scale. Then this primary sin determines the fate of man's spirit as well.

A polarization within the Absolute takes shape here. A life beyond all possible existences, about which nothing is known, is an unknown God. Within it appears life and also light, the great Second who in the realm of life, within itself and out of itself, gives shape to

14. Ginza, *Der Schatz oder das Große Buch der Mandäer*, trans. Mark Lidzbarski (Göttingen: Vandenhoeck & Ruprecht, 1925), 328.

15. Viz. Plato's *soma-sema* (the body is a prison).

16. Jakob Boehme (1575–1624), a German, Protestant mystical philosopher seems to have known Gnostic literature because he explains the birth of Sophia as the projection or imagination of the Primary Base. The idea that the polarity of good and evil is already present in God also appears in Boehme.

the primary form of all possible existences (forms of mind), and then feels a yearning to declare them; therefore, it creates another pole, the creator *demiourgos* (will or want) who announces this yearning as the world, and projects light (or a part of it) into the world out of which the above mentioned cosmic drama develops.

Although not in accordance with the norms of ancient philosophy or science, the mythological ideas of Gnosticism present a kind of symbolic, quasi-metaphysical system. Thus we can rely on general ontology when trying to explore the logic of Gnostic Sophia, which also means that, prior to classical cultures or in parallel to them, outstanding minds of ancient oriental cultures already reached abstract generalizations, only they recorded their findings in a system of signs different from our own.

The descent of the Logos is described by Gnosticism through an image that reflects itself, standing in front of its own imagination. This image or icon of the Logos, like the female partner of man, is Sophia, divine Wisdom. Sophia is the copy of Logos, the imprisoned light out of Logos in the world for whom Logos will arrive as redeemer, and where darkness or depth is the world of time and space.

Logos, that is life without its armory (without primary matter) already as Sophia, or as a trapped "caveman" (= macrocosm), struggles in swirls because it is controlled by drunkenness and confusion that has been triggered by the wine of the unknown. The wine of drunkenness in the mind serves to erase the knowledge of alienation in the world so that the spirit gains an experience of itself as belonging to this world. As a result, the spirit becomes insensitive to its primary origin and listens to the voices of and observes the laws of the world, while confused utterances come from its lips.[17]

Contrary to all this, Gnosis or *manda* (primary knowledge) survives in the world as *Sophia perennis* (viz. *perennitas*) whose primary knowledge awakens man exalted by a sober drunkenness to his knowledge of origin again. Here is how the 11th Ode of Solomon captures this paradox: "Speaking waters of the spring of the Lord flooded my lips. I drank and got drunken from the waters of immor-

17. Hans Jonas, *Die mythologische Gnosis* (München: Barth, 1998), 56.

tality. However, my drunkenness was not of ignorance, but instead, I have left nothingness behind."

We have already discussed that the question of dualism or monism in Gnosticism might be settled resting on Mandaean thoughts first of all—which argue for monism—or on what, from the perspective of a comparative history of religions, we could term a primary monist revelation. However, orientation toward Greek and Manichean Gnosticism will reveal a dualistic character. The analysis of the notion of the world in relation to Gnostic mythology is closely connected to our present inquiry.

As light, the second life has a counterpart identical with itself (a confused worldly light, a light observing itself in a reflection: in Sophia). Likewise does the third, the *demiourgos*, have its identical counterpart: a creative will in the world, an anti-god construing a specific world, an anti-god who creates worlds and false gods out of the armory of light and who is presented in a feminine aspect in Mandaean texts. This demonic, imprisoning feminineness is the opposite of the feminineness awaiting in Sophia to be rescued; but since both are aspects of the same feminineness, of the manifested world, they are ultimately and in their essence one and the same. Thus it is clear that at every level of Gnosticism we face a quasi-dualism which in the end can be retraced to a single point.

Here is an excerpt from a Manichean cosmogony: "And they [the Living Soul and its follower by name] wandered deep into the region of darkness and they found the caveman lost in darkness. Then the Living Soul had shrieked and its voice sounded like a sharp sword. [...] And the Call and the Response guiding each other had risen to the Mother of Life and the Living Soul. The Living Soul dressed the call, while the Mother of Life dressed the response as their beloved son."[18]

In Manichean symbolism, the Living Soul is nothing else than Logos, that is the life and light imprisoned by the world who now appears as a herald with a mission to wake up the caveman, the Adam of macrocosm. The Mother of Life, on the other hand, might be a step of pre-cosmic divine transfigurations or the feminine

---

18. Ginza, *Schatz*, 95.

aspect of light imprisoned in the world: Sophia. The response to be given to the call coming from Logos is clothed and delivered to Logos by this feminine quality, clothed in heavenly clothes, in light.[19]

In conclusion: Gnosticism is an overall form of speculation concerning the Logos where the role of Logos is bound within God (theologically), in cosmogony-cosmology, and in soteriology; but its feminine aspect, Sophia or the World-Soul, also appears, who represents the maternal face of the Divine. Besides this polarity, the polarity of good and evil appears as well in some varieties of Gnosticism as an off-shoot of monism and monotheism, while in other varieties a sharp dualism dominates.

On the basis of this overview of Gnosticism an exciting further inquiry may address how a polytheism or, from a more orthodox perspective, the idea of the multitude of forms can be rehabilitated in a (at its root) monotheistic system. For in Gnosticism gods are none other than guards of the spheres or *aions*: personifications of particles, of the laws of nature, of functions of knowledge, and even symbols of specific spheres. These guards have clothed man's spirit in a body, and they earn the respect of the spirit while it sleeps in a body, but the spirit must meet the guards after its awakening on its way to God and then defeat them as forms of its own imagination.

Although Gnosticism is only a side-track in antiquity alongside classical Greek thought or the notions of the Old Testament and the New Testament, it still carries interesting illuminations connected to our study. The ideas that duality or *dyas* grows out of One-ness, that this duality takes form in the third, and, further, that the Absolute is polarized perhaps as a step toward a male-female duality or the opposites of good and evil are all present already.[20] And although Sophia here is secondary to Logos, the pair of Logos and Sophia is a new variety of the same *hieros gamos* that we have seen in Greek philosophy.

---

19. Viz.: Rev 12:1, "The woman clothed with the sun."

20. That a polarity of good and evil and especially the source of evil would be present in divine being does not appear in Christian tradition. However, whether a feminine being may be present in it is the main query of our dissertation.

5

The Cosmic World-Soul

A s WE HAVE seen thus far, the World-Soul (the Gaia goddess in myths; *nous, logos, pneuma, psyche, sophia* in Greek philosophy) is a crucial notion of ancient times. Christian thinkers considered the myth of Gaia and the motif of the World-Soul to be pantheistic. However, the idea of a Divine Spirit that governs the universe survived also in medieval theology, for example, in the proof, starting from finality, for the existence of God in Aquinas. From the end of the Middle Ages and the beginning of the Renaissance, numerous insights came forward regarding how the ancients regarded the living nature of the cosmos. Let us turn, then, to the later history of the World-Intelligence, the World-Soul.

Theologian, mathematician, bishop, and cardinal Nicholas of Cusa is an important figure at the birth of the early modern period. Karl Jaspers has called him the composer of the great metaphysics of his times. Cusa says that man is a microcosm and, consequently, the image and likeness of the macrocosm. The universe, however, is not God himself for Cusa. All parts of the universe are permeated by the divine Spirit. In this sense it is an organically constructed cosmos. Here we should note Cusa's doctrine of *coincidentia oppositorum*. This is the idea that God is present in the minor in the same manner as in the major. The universe is, therefore, a self-existing personality; the Kingdom on a large scale. Cusa thought barbaric the idea that the universe consists of dead matter.

It is well known that Nicholas Copernicus as well as Johann Kepler reinterpreted the thought of Aristarchus of Samos (320 BC). Aristarchus had proposed the heliocentric hypothesis of the relative movements of the sun and planets. Similarly, Kepler said that the planets move in ellipses, with the sun as their focus. It is worth

49

mentioning that Copernicus also maintained the theory of the spheres, where everything revolves round the sun, and also held that the cosmos is a living being. In Kepler, however, the thought of the identification of cosmos with living being is very important, as he wrote, "*Mundus est imago Dei corporea*" (the world is the corporeal image of God). Beyond the visible and intelligible, psychic processes lie concealed.

Giordano Bruno took a further step. He said that the sun moves, and the fixed stars also revolve around, other foci. In a way similar to Plato's description of the World-Soul, he called the universe the Great Soul, which has a leading principle of life: "The moving principle, the soul, and the moved, the body (the universe), give the possibility of motion." All smaller and bigger beings have an "inner moving-principle, own nature, individual soul, and individual intelligence."[1] It is erroneous to believe that Bruno had a merely pantheistic view of the motion of world-being. Although he speaks of world-individuals, he confessed that the World-Soul is not God, but a spiritual essence.

In the 18th and 19th centuries, the idea of a World-Soul came into view again. The first proponent of this view was Friedrich Ernst Daniel Schleiermacher, who said that the world is an all-embracing organism that comprises both nature and intellect. Friedrich Wilhelm Schelling argued that the beginning of organic life is not dead matter, but life. For them, the whole world is a pan-organism, comprising both the organic and the inorganic. The universe is furthermore shaped by the Absolute, that is, by the most perfect organic being; and it is permeated by the World-Soul, which maintains the continuity of inorganic life, while at the same time forming one single organism out of the totality of nature. Schelling developed his philosophy of nature as an antithesis to the mechanical understanding of nature.

The idea of a World-Soul is evident also in the works of Goethe. The title to one of his most important poems, *Die Weltseele*—which was inspired by Schelling—confirms this. We find in this poem the beautiful line: "And every tiny grain of dust is living."

---

1. Giordano Bruno, *La Cena de le Cineri*, V, T. 93.

The Cosmic World-Soul

At the turn of the twentieth century, physicist and philosopher Gustav Theodor Fechner developed a very passionate world-view that takes as its main thesis the notion that "Earth is a creature like our body." Fechner later confessed he had been deeply influenced by both Solovyov and Teilhard de Chardin.

The Eternal Feminine in Teilhard de Chardin

We come now to the views of Pierre Teilhard de Chardin. Teilhard was born in Landsitz, Sarcenat in 1881, and died in New York in 1955. Here we will analyze his writings from the viewpoint of sophiology. His ideas are particularly interesting since he says that the World Soul is not only an entelechy governing the world, but a personal reality. As Adolf Haas has remarked: "According to Teilhard the Universe is personal. It may well seem that universality and personality are irreconcilable, but for Teilhard it is not impossible."[2] Moreover, Teilhard also says that this ultimate, personal principle is a mother, that it has a feminine character, or in other words, represents the Eternal Feminine. Finally, Teilhard, influenced by Jung's theory of the animus-anima, adds that the Eternal Feminine's male partner is the cosmic Christ. He writes,

> there has emerged [in the man of today] the demand of the contact of Jesus and the world. Christ and the World Soul are not opposite, independent realities *in natura rerum*, but one of them is the focus wherein we can recognize the other. The World Soul is an indispensable reality—in a certain sense even more directly than Christ—since Christ has to exert his influence through the World Soul. The World Soul—which coexists with the Logos—is at the same time the point of support for incarnation. She supplies the prepared matter, which is suitable to establish the Mystical Body. In a fully integral and authentic Christianity the World Soul and Christ are not opposed.[3]

---

2. Adolf Haas, *Teilhard de Chardin-Lexikon,* bd. 2. I–Z (Freiburg: Amazon, 1971), 244.
3. Chardin, *Frühe Schriften* (Freiburg/München: Verlag Karl Alber, 1968), 217.

It is worthwhile to recall here the main passages from his *Hymn to the Eternal Feminine*,[4] because it comprises almost all the main points of the essay:

> When the world was born, I came into being.[5] Before the centuries were made, I issued from the hand of God—half-formed, yet destined to grow in beauty from age to age, the handmaid of his work.
>
> Everything in the universe is made by union and generation—by the coming together of elements that seek out one another, melt together two by two, and are born again in a third.
>
> God instilled me into the initial multiple as a force of condensation and concentration.
>
> In me is seen that side of beings by which they are joined as one, in me the fragrance that makes them hasten together and leads them, freely and passionately, along their road to unity.
>
> Through me, all things have their movement and are made to work as one.
>
> I am the beauty running through the world, to make it associate in ordered groups: the ideal held up before the world to make it ascend.
>
> I am the essential Feminine.
>
> In me, the soul is at work to sublimate the body—Grace to divinize the soul.
>
> If God, then, was to be able to emerge from himself, he had first to lay a pathway of desire before his feet, he had to spread before him a sweet savor of beauty.
>
> It was then that he caused me to rise up, a luminous mist hanging over the abyss—between the earth and himself—that, in me, he might dwell among you.
>
> Lying between God and the earth, as a zone of mutual attraction, I draw them both together in a passionate union.
>
> —until the meeting takes place in me, in which the generation

---

4. Pierre Teilhard de Chardin, *Writings in Time of War*, trans. Rene Hague (New York: Harper and Row, 1968), 191–202. Also included in *The Heavenly Country: Primary Sources, Poetry, and Critical Essays on Sophiology*, ed. Michael Martin (Kettering, OH: Angelico Press, 2016), 158–65.

5. Sir 24:9.

and plenitude of Christ are consummated throughout the centuries.

I am the Church, the bride of Christ.
I am Mary the Virgin, mother of all human kind.

I am the Eternal Feminine.

Henri de Lubac, in his commentary on the poem, remarks that in Teilhard's vision Mary is the universal creation. Christ and Mary are the accomplished center of the new world. Teilhard sets up the claim for overcoming the male-centered conception of God with the help of the reimagination of the Eternal Feminine.

According to Thomas Schipflinger, Teilhard in his *Poem to the World Soul* searches for the necessary connection of Christ with the world, and understands it to be the unity of Christ and the World Soul. The ancient insight concerning nature becomes realized by the mother nature: the World Soul is God's lover. According to Proverbs 8:32, Sophia is the lover of Yahweh as well as his fellow creator. The world is the fabric of Sophia, and the incarnated Sophia is the Virgin Mary. According to the medieval adage *Per Mariam ad Iesum*, Mary (in our present context the World Soul) leads to Christ.

The notion of a World Soul appeared for the Greeks and other natural religions in a polytheistic context. Here it became possible to give a theological interpretation to the notion. We see in Teilhard's hymn that the World Soul is Sophia-Mary (usually put Mary-Sophia by analogy to Jesus-Christ: i.e., human nature first, divine second). The sophianic understanding of the World Soul makes possible conceiving nature religiously rather than in an exploitive manner. Since nature is the body of Sophia, it becomes the subject of affection. Femininity has received a new meaning through the Eternal Feminine.

Through the awareness of the Eternal Feminine, the Church receives a new insight. As Teilhard remarks, our task is to know the World Soul and to dedicate our life to her; in other words, to work and live is a way worthy of her. Teilhard does not consider the World Soul to be a goddess; he emphasizes her createdness. On the other hand, she is numinous, cosmic, universal; a personal entelechy, a proto-idea, like the Hokmah of the Old Testament or its equivalent in other world religions, which have also arrived at the recognition of the notion of the mother of the world, to the great mother.

6

Hokmah-Sophia
in Scripture

Wisdom Books

S O FAR we have summed up the concepts of the principle of wisdom followed by philosophies and belief systems generally
peripheral to Judeo-Christianity. Yet, from our perspective, an
extremely important question concerns what the Bible says about
this principle and perhaps about God's maternal face. First we will
examine the teachings of the Old Testament on this topic. A wonderful source, the wisdom books, have thus far been effectively
neglected from this perspective by traditional inquiries, yet they
provide a definition of the concept of Wisdom (*Hokmah*).

According to Catholic theology the wisdom books of the Bible
include five books: the Book of Job, Ecclesiastes, Proverbs, the Book
of Jesus the Son of Sirach, and the Wisdom of Solomon. Some edi-
tions change the order of the last two books for the sake of chronology and many theologians include the Song of Songs in this group,
partly because of its theme and partly because Jewish tradition
holds it to be the work of the same King Solomon as the other Wisdom books (except Job).

Wisdom and Sirach are included in the Catholic and Orthodox
canon, while Jewish tradition, despite the inclusion of the books in
the Septuagint, does not regard them as canonical. As a result, the
Reformation also rejected these books. Nevertheless, Luther translated them and personally regarded them with high esteem.

According to contemporary research, parts of Proverbs were

recorded around 930 BC, although it reached its present form only around 330 BC. Job was finalized around 400 BC, Ecclesiastes around 260 BC, Sirach around 180 BC, and Wisdom circa 110 BC.[1]

The literature of wisdom offers a summary of its main theme: "I want to declare what wisdom is and how it came about and I do not intend to conceal any secrets from you. I wish to follow its traces from the beginning of creation, I would like to promote it and will not hold back anything of truth" (Wisdom 6:22).

We see a progression through the wisdom literature. The first three books explain life and salvation in the dimension of earthly life, while the last two assume a world beyond. The authors in the latter case adapt Egyptian thought through Babylonian mediation to a monotheist context. Sophia is already presented in a cosmological role in Proverbs, perhaps on the basis of the Isis-cult, since this influence is earlier than the influence exerted on the Greeks (viz. Platonism and Neoplatonism).[2] Wisdom, the last among the wisdom books, shows a turning point: its horizon is eternity. It introduces the idea of the immortality of the spirit and the rewards to be acquired in eternity. This book, being the last in chronology in the Old Testament, breaks with the time-frame and spatiality of the other books and attributes to Wisdom the ability to surpass the boundaries of eternity. This fundamentally fresh good news revises the notions formerly held on life, happiness, and truth, and offers a new solution for previous problems, foreshadowing the good news about the arrival of the Lord Jesus.

Wisdom was written in the Hellenic center of Alexandria around 100 BC. The Hebrew *Hokmah* here is rendered as *Sophia* since this book of the Septuagint was originally written in Greek. Here Sophia is already a mediator between Yahweh, the world, and man; or, to use Greek terminology, Sophia co-exists with *nous* and *logos* and in many respects resembles both Demeter and Isis of late Greek mythology.

Despite the resemblances, however, the author of Wisdom is an

---

1. *St. Jerome Bible*, 504, 645, 674, 690, 711.
2. Schipflinger, *Sophia*, 27.

independent writer inspired by God who is aware of these parallels and who points out that all former similarities were only preparations for revelation. He records how wisdom has influenced other peoples, "Passing into holy souls from age to age, she produces friends of God and prophets" (7:27).

What we see here is a kind of ecumenism of the Old Testament. Although the author shows us the imperfections of Greek philosophy and other religions, he rejects the Hellenized cults of Egyptian gods and at the same time recognizes the values of other religions. He creates a synthesis between Jewish tradition and the ideas of other peoples and sums up what he believes true and fine in them all.

There are many similarities between the period at the turn of the second century BC and our contemporary world, the turning point of the Second Vatican Council, the doctrines of *Gaudium et Spes*, and the aims of the Council of Non-Christians among them. The synthesis of the former period is an example for our age. This synthesis validated that the preparation for the good news of Christ had been completed and was ready to be spread all over the world. Let us note that this last stroke of the brush in the Old Testament establishes the notion of wisdom.

Personal Wisdom

The notion of wisdom goes through development in the wisdom books. As *sophia* in Greek, so *hokmah* in the beginning signified human wisdom and skill. Wisdom was a virtue by which one can acquire happiness. But here it is not so much the result of man's striving as in the Greek concept; rather, it is the divine gift of mercy. Furthermore, only God can operate with it, thus it is the essence of God. It has always existed, even before God created the world; wisdom is somehow God's co-creator, His faithful consultant, His bride and fiancée (viz. Prov 8:22–31; Wisdom 8:3–4, 9:4).

Some characteristics of Wisdom are already revealed in the Book of Job (viz. 15:1; 12:23–26). Wisdom is not personified in Ecclesiastes; rather, practical advice is provided for the reader. Proverbs, on the other hand, designates Wisdom as our great teacher and guide to happiness, describing her as the royal host on the feast of a happy life (8:22–31). In Sirach, the personal character of wisdom is revisited: it stems from the lips of God, it rules the world and its peoples, and it accepts Israel as His own people. Wisdom's role as a universal organizing principle is also highlighted; it operates as the law of the world, which is identical with the law of God, the Torah. As a result, the Torah is the road to happiness, although here it is only treated to an aspect of our temporary and current world (viz. Sirach 24:1–12, 23–26).

Wisdom in the book of Wisdom is the (female) counsellor of creation who knows the writings and selects among them those to be communicated to God; she both departs from and is destined to God; she is the road from God overarching creation and the road that leads the created world back to God. Furthermore, she is a mother and "the first author of beauty" (Wisdom 13:3), the spirit of the world (Wisdom 9:9–11, 7:22, and 8:1, wherein she beneficially manages the affairs of the universe). The role of Wisdom as co-creator appears elsewhere in the Old Testament, for instance, in the "creation psalm": "How great are your works, O Lord? In wisdom you have made them all" (103:24).

The Book of Wisdom is the ultimate revelation of Sophia in the Old Testament: her secretive, personal character is here unfolded. We learn that she originates from God, and she is a relation of God bearing divine characteristics; she is with God as His companion and counsellor on the throne. She is described in poetic yet unambiguous style: the text moves from her allegorical personification to the hypostasizing of her essence (viz. Wisdom 7:25–28; 8:3–4; 9:4).

The holy author also describes Wisdom's relation to the universe: she is the creator of the universe, a pure spiritual force that permeates, animates, and rejuvenates everything. "An intelligent and holy, unique and manifold, fine and eloquent, swift and flawless spirit is present in her; [...] she is benevolent and friendly, [...] omnipotent and omniscient, she wades through any substances [...] because she is the breath of God's power and she drips from the pure glory of God. There is no stain in her because she emanates from eternal light, she is the clear image of God's superiority and a mirror of His goodness" (Wisdom 7:22–26). Let us note the details of the relation of Wisdom and the (holy) Spirit.

Wisdom is the highest cosmic, spiritual being; she is created by God and bestowed with all abilities to become what she is—a participant in the act of creation, the primal idea and universal *entelecheia* of creation, the heart and soul of the world:

> I came out of the mouth of the most High, the firstborn before all
>   creatures:
> I made that in the heavens there should rise light that never fail-
>   eth, and as a cloud I covered all the earth:
> I dwelt in the highest places, and my throne is in a pillar of a
>   cloud.
> I alone have compassed the circuit of heaven, and have penetrated
>   into the bottom of the deep, and have walked in the waves of
>   the sea. (Sirach 24:5–8)

The concept of a World-Soul necessitates the idea of *arche* (Hebrew—*résit*), which is not only a beginning but also a primal principle. "And thy wisdom with thee, which knoweth thy works, which then also was present when thou madest the world" (Wisdom 9:9). These words seem to imply that Sophia had existed before the birth of time and before the world was created or even that she is an eternal being, a divine person. The Old Testament does not provide a clear answer to such a query. In the light of the New Testament, however, one can phrase the question as to whether this pre-existent Sophia might be identified as Logos or even the Holy Spirit.

Yet Sophia is connected not only to God and the world, but also to man, since God loves her so much that she is endowed with the dignity of co-creation, so much so that she becomes the source of every life and rebirth, of healing, fruition, and perfection. She takes care of men of any nation and, as we have seen, enables them to become friends with God, to become prophets, religious teachers, and leaders.

Beyond these roles the motherly character of Sophia is also apparent. And although in Hebrew the gender of words is not always clear, as opposed to Indo-European languages, and often only the context reveals the gender of a given word, we can ascertain that *hokmah* is feminine just as in Greek (*Sophia*) or in Latin (*sapientia*) and, *nomen est omen*, as so often, the linguistic form determines the ontological content of the word.[3]

The feminine or motherly character of Hokmah (Sophia) is expressed most clearly in Sirach: "I am the mother of fair love, and of fear, and of knowledge, and of holy hope" (24:24). This motherhood occasionally appears in symbols: "I, wisdom, have poured out rivers" (Sirach 24:40); and most often appears in the symbol of a nurturing mother: "Come over to me, all ye that desire me, and be filled with my fruits" (24:26). "For my spirit is sweet above honey, and my inheritance above honey and the honeycomb" (24:27) and "They that eat me, shall yet hunger: and they that drink me, shall yet thirst" (24:29). The last image foreshadows Christ and the Eucharist (viz. John 6:54) just as does the confession of Wisdom: "In me is all grace of the way and of the truth, in me is all hope of life and of virtue" (Sirach 24:25). Christ will announce himself as "the way, the truth and the life."

Often what we see, however, is a kind of *hieros gamos*, a "marital" relation between Yahweh and his people in which Sophia, as the bride, personifies the people of Israel: "I took root in an honorable people, and in the portion of my God his inheritance, and my abode is in the full assembly of saints" (Sirach 24:16). In this respect, Wisdom foreshadows the bride of Christ, the Church (Ephesians 5). Perhaps this tradition has survived in the Church as, until very recently, it assigned readings for the feasts of the Virgin Mary from the wisdom books on the basis of Mary being the personified mother of the Church. This aspect points toward the mariological dimension of Sophia.

Independently of this collective personification (contextualized with the people of Israel), Sophia often appears as the *Amon* or love of Yahweh, as testimony of the bonds of a most superior, sacred marriage: "I was with him forming all things: and was delighted every day, playing before him at all times" (Prov 8:30); "She glorifies her nobility by being conversant with God: yea and the Lord of all things has loved her" (Wisdom 8:3).

---

3. The Arabic word for *Hokma* (*Hikma*) is also feminine.

Hokmah-Sophia in Scripture

Although strictly speaking the Song of Songs is not one of the wisdom books, and its central theme is not wisdom, its semblance with Proverbs is striking in its exalted depiction of love and matrimony wherein wisdom is the bride and, further, in the relationship of Yahweh and His love, Sophia (viz. Prov 6).

Ultimately, both in the Song of Songs and the books of wisdom, a fiancé-bride relationship appears between God and Sophia on the one hand, and between God and the chosen nation on the other. This had already been the key to explicating the Song of Songs in the Jewish tradition which, in turn, was transplanted into the Christian faith, which is why the dominant interpretation of the text has always revolved around the love-relation of Christ and the Church.

In this sense, the Song of Songs is an integral part of Sophia literature. It sums up the love between God and the world, mankind, that is the chosen people, or, from another perspective, the love of Christ and Sophia. Yet, the interpretation according to which the idea in Genesis 2:23–24 is developed into poetry here, as at similar points in the literature of wisdom, holds that this is how God becomes represented in the unity and duality of man and woman. Other books of the Bible inform us of this holy nuptial as well. This is what Jeremiah has to say, for instance, "O virgin of Israel: you shall again be adorned with your timbrels, and shall go forth in the dances of them that make merry" (31:4). This hierogamic relationship has its parallels in the history of other religions, but, as we have made it clear, this is not a parallel of effect and consequence, much rather the manifestation of a common human spirit.

Sophia for Philo of Alexandria

Philo lived from 13 BC to AD 45, a time contemporaneous with the birth of Christianity. He knew ancient Greek thought, the teachings of Gnosticism, and Egyptian religious wisdom. He tried to mediate between these philosophies and the Old Testament, and, in fact, his ideas lie between the Old and the New Testament understandings of Sophia as well. Research demonstrates that Philo, as did St. Paul and the Church Fathers, identifies Logos as Sophia. However, similarities and parallels do not result in a common identity: man and the

61

world have the similar tasks and modes of appearance, but this semblance does not mean they are totally identical.

We have familiarized ourselves with the fundamental vocabulary of Sophia in the chapter on the wisdom of antiquity: *logos, idea, nous, demiourgos, eikon, pneuma, psyche, sophia.* In the age of Philo the principles of the Stoics dominated philosophy and the foremost Hellenic idea became the Logos. This Hellenic background prompts Philo to identify Logos with Sophia verbally, but not in its essential reality. This was also the reason for the patristic process of identification.[4] Another reason for Philo, just as for the Jews and Christians, was the domineering patriarchal mentality of the period.

As we have already mentioned, there are texts in the literature of wisdom that may have served as a foundation for equating the concepts of Logos and Sophia. The parallel of "word" and "wisdom" (*davar* and *hokmah*) appears in a number of places, for example in the Book of Wisdom: "God of my fathers, and Lord of mercy, who has made all things with your word, And by your wisdom have appointed man" (9:1–2). This parallel may have been phrased for the sake of diction or rhetoric, or it may signify a total equality, but it can also mark the complementary, polar feature of the two elements. The Old Testament records that the word of God (*davar, memra Yahweh*) created the world (viz. Psalms 33:6; Isaiah 55:11), but often the same act is carried out by *Hokmah* or by *Ruah Yahweh* (the spirit of God); as a result, the two sides can be seen as complements of each other.[5]

Even though Philo often sees Logos and Sophia as equals, sometimes he treats Sophia as an independent entity.[6] He depicts her with images familiar from the literature of wisdom: the house of truth, food and drink, girl, the bride, or even the spouse of God, His co-creator, the mother of the world. He construes a hierogamic relationship between God and Sophia:

---

4. Jean Daniélou, *Platonisme et Theologie mystique* (Paris: Aubert, 1954), 165.
5. Burton Lee Mack, *Logos und Sophia: Untersuchungen zur Weisheitstheologie im hellenistischen Judentum* (Göttingen: Vandenhoeck & Ruprecht, 1975), 94.
6. Bernhard Lang, *Frau Weisheit, Deutung einer biblische Gestalt* (Düsseldorf: Patmos, 1975), 161.

Demiourgos, who created our universe, can be described as the father of the First creature, but also as a mother, since she is the wisdom (*epistheme*) of the inseminator, she lives with God and she gives birth to creation, yet not in any human way. She accommodated the seed of God and with His only beloved son, our world, as a ripe fruit, and gave life to it in labor. According to the writings she tears herself away from the divine dance with the following self-confession: "God created me as the first of His works and He founded me before time."[7]

Philo concludes that "Thus necessarily every creature must be younger than the mother and nurse maid of the universe."[8] The concept of the first-born of creatures is confirmed.

Sophia for Philo is the primary principle (*arche*) of the world. According to Spenneut, Philo used the following passages from the literature of wisdom as his sources: "The Lord possessed me in the beginning [*arche*] of his ways" (Prov 8:22); "I was with him forming all things" (Prov 8: 30); "is the worker [*technitis*] of all things" (Wisdom 7:22a); "For it is she that teacheth the knowledge of God, and is the chooser of his works" (Wisdom 8:4); "The Lord by wisdom [*boe-hokma, te Sophia*] founded the earth" (Prov 3:19); "She reaches therefore from end to end mightily, and orders all things sweetly" (Wisdom 8:1). In light of this, the first line of the Bible may ring a new tone: "In the beginning (*boe-resit*) God created the sky and the earth" (Gen 1:1). Perhaps this also means that God created everything by *arche*, that is, by Sophia.[9]

In Philo's interpretation the same is expressed as follows: Yahweh created Sophia, she is thus the daughter of God, *arche* or the beginning of creation, mother of the cosmos. The Lord creates the cosmos through Sophia. In this way, the cosmos is the Son whose Father is Yahweh and whose mother is Sophia.[10] Following the Platonic school, Philo believes this cosmos consists of ideas and matter in which the cosmos materialized. For the idea of cosmos he bor-

7. Philo here refers to Proverbs 6:22.
8. Philo, *De ebrietate*, 31.
9. Michel Spenneut, "Le stoicisme des Pères de l'Eglise," in *Patristica Sorbonnensia* (Paris: Seuil, 1957), 45.
10. Philo, *Ebrietate*, 32.

rows the expression of Stoicism, *logos noetos*, while its visible manifestation he calls *logos aesthetos*. This is how he incorporates the
idea of Logos in his own cosmology. Accordingly, the idea of cosmos is inherent in the idea of ideas: in Sophia, who comes indirectly
from Yahweh. The relation of *logos noetos* and *aesthetos* he expresses
with the symbolic relationship of mother and son. Yahweh passed
on the motherly task of taking care of the cosmos to Sophia. This is
why Philo calls her mother, nurturer, and *Amme*.[11]

He may have borrowed the motherly and nurturing character
from the figure of the goddess Isis, who, as Sophia, "fills heaven and
earth with her beauty [...], is great in the sky and mighty on earth
[...], everything came from her and the universe is alive and maintained by her."[12] According to Philo, Sophia passes many aspects of
this role onto the Logos, as a mother to her son. The Son naturally
takes after her and the Father. The eikon or image of Sophia and so
the image of Yahweh, is the Sun and the Light, a resemblance to
Yahweh and Sophia. "God is Light [...] and thus Logos is also Light
being totally permeated by God."[13] And just as Sophia, Logos is also
wisdom, *arche*, a beginning: *"deuteros theos"* (= the second god).[14]

One could continue with examples, but this much will be sufficient to justify that Philo transfers the features of Sophia (and so of
Hokmah of the Old Testament) to Logos, but only as a second step.
He borrowed mythological and cosmological concepts and images
from Greek and Egyptian culture and incorporated them in his
sophiology. However, he replaces truths unacceptable to him, such
as the Stoic idea of the eternity of matter, with the concept of creation.

He also borrows from the Greeks the concept of *demiourgos* or
the primary principle of the world (*idea idearum*) as well as the
concept of a World-Spirit, but he clears them of pantheist and ema-
native influences as much as possible. This is how he incorporates
the concepts of *demiourgos, idea, eikon, pneuma, logos noetos,* and

11. Philo, "Quaestiones in Genesim," in *Ebrietate* 31.
12. Lee Mack, *Logos*, 157.
13. Philo, *De somniis* I, 75, viz. Rev 1:4; 1:9.
14. Philo, *Fuga*, 101, 108.

aesthetos in his philosophy. His style and mode of expression are Greek, very close to Hellenism, yet his intellectual basis and his objectives remain consistently those of a Jewish tradition. The *Lexikon für Theologie und Kirche*[15] describes him as someone who left behind magnificent ideas on God and the world and these ideas greatly influenced such Christian authors and Church Fathers as Clement of Alexandria and Origen.

From the perspective of our dissertation, it is necessary to view the scholarly assumption that Philo considered Logos and Sophia identical as incorrect: Sophia merely transferred the attributes of Wisdom to Logos (as to her Son). The concept of equalization, however, became a kind of *theologoumenon* in later Christian trinitology, but today such ideas are considered faulty and obsolete. Only subsequent research on Philo has brought along a proper assessment of him, paralleling reassessments of the concept of Sophia by a number of authors, philosophers, visionaries, and theologians, by St. Augustine, Hildegard of Bingen, Bonaventura, Heinrich Suso, Jakob Boehme, Gottfried Arnold, Solovyov, Florensky, Bulgakov, and Teilhard de Chardin, among others. Philo's teaching is an important contribution to the picture drawn by the Old Testament on Sophia, the divine wisdom.

Hokmah-Sophia-Shekinah in the Kabbalah

Hokmah-Sophia of the Old Testament survives in the Kabbalah as well. In the traditions of both the Talmud and the Kabbalah, the mysterious figure of *Shekinah* plays an important role: "Shekinah is the personification, presence and hypostasy of God in the world; a concept which the Jews have carried along through the storms and fateful turns of history for two thousand years."[16] Jewish theology and philosophy of the Middle Ages considered Shekinah the representation of God's glory and grandeur: created, but first in line. Although many Jewish scholars see Shekinah as a male entity, upon

---

15. Ed. Herbert Vorgrimler (München: Herder, 1965).

16. Gerschom Scholem, "Von der Mystischen Gestalt der Gottheit," in *Studien zu Grundbegriffen der Kabbalah* (Frankfurt: Suhrkamp, 1977), 136.

elaboration it appears she is the mother, a matron, the queen of all created beings, our road to the king.[17] Occasionally, she is a maiden whom God sent into the world: the daughter, the sister, the bride, the close associate of the king (God), a mediator through whom the glory of God becomes accessible.

The gender of the word "*Shekinah*" (as of "*Hokmah*") is feminine. Her maternal or feminine character is often dressed in symbols: "the fragrant fine vessel of the king," "a precious vessel which the king offers to his son," "the throne of God," "the house of God," Jerusalem, the congregation of Israel, "*malkut*" or kingdom: the presence of God's reign. Moses ben Nachma (†1270) identifies her with the tenth sephiroth. For others she is the sister of Abraham, and her name, *Bakol*, means to be present in all—a primary principle, an *arche* who lives with everything but also stands above everything. *Bakol* also means "blessing" and thus Shekinah is a blessing for all of us. Her manifestations, according to the traditions of the Kabbalah are Sarah, Rebecca, and Rachel.[18]

The Kabbalah extends the concept of Shekinah to metaphysics. Perhaps on the basis of Gnostic or Neoplatonic tradition, in the Kabbalah everything in creation receives its form and shape from her: "She is the form which transcends all forms, in which all unique shapes had already been formed in their specific individuality."[19] What we have here is a variety of the ancient hylemorphism, but spanning the whole of the cosmos: "Forms are dresses of Shekinah. When God views the world, He does not see His creation directly but in a form in which Shekinah presents and dresses them for Him."[20] The theme of reflection in this text had already appeared with Hokmah in the Old Testament and in Gnostic literature.

To sum up her cosmological role: Shekinah is the lady of the world, the angel of God, *Beth-El*, the abode of God. Yet she is also a participant of a nuptial ceremony: the bride at a wedding, the congregation of Israel. She is eternal femininity: *ha issa ha elyona* (heav-

---

17. Ibid.
18. Schipflinger continues: Radha, Tara, Isis, Tao... Viz. *Sophia*, 173.
19. Ibid., 174.
20. Ibid.

enly woman), woman of light, the sum of everything that is feminine in the world.[21] The Kabbalah has a term for *hieros gamos*: *Civvuga kaddis* or sacred nuptial. Yahweh and Shekinah, as king and queen, sit side by side. Somehow the nuptial or union takes place within God: *jichuda*, *zivvuga*, says the Kabbalah, perhaps following the model in the Song of Songs (viz., for example, 2:6).[22]

Thus it is apparent that Shekinah is no different from Sophia: created, but the first among created beings. She is the immanence of God, she personifies His presence in the world, yet, at the same time, she is also transcendent and a precondition to the immanent unity of the world. The world, nature, and anything created is the appearance of *Shekinah-Hokmah*, her body, her clothes, while she is the innermost *entelecheia*. Like *Bakol*, she is the mother and soul of the entire cosmos, a heavenly madonna, eternally feminine.

Shekinah-Sophia is likewise the innermost cosmic law who was embodied in the Torah. She is the lady of the world, the World-Soul, a prime foundation, the ancient principle of life; she bears a preliminary image and the inner rational seed of everything. Furthermore, the modern scientific view that the universe is a single organism permeated by rationality, spirituality, and subjectivity points toward an ancient maternal principle and it could gain new impulses from the Kabbalah, especially if this principle is identified as Sophia, the primary model.

The New Testament on Sophia: A Cursory Note

On the basis of what has been said thus far, one might query what the New Testament has to say on Divine Wisdom. Since for us, Christians, what the Lord Jesus teaches us is distinctly important. Relying on conventional knowledge or even on the church fathers who identified Sophia as Logos, one hardly finds any texts on Sophia.

Among the few references is the statement of Jesus: "wisdom is justified by her children" (Matt 11:19). Wisdom here is expressed as a virtue of man. Many details from the literature of wisdom are echoed

21. Ibid., 177.
22. Ibid., 179.

in the writings of St. Paul, but for him wisdom is more like a rhetorical turn or a feature of God at best: "O the depth of the riches of the wisdom and of the knowledge of God! How incomprehensible are his judgments, and how unsearchable his ways! For who hath known the mind of the Lord? Or who hath been his counsellor?" (Rom 11:33–34). Here appears an important detail: Wisdom as counsellor.

Yet, Paul guides us on and gives us a key to further texts when he presents the features of the church: it is the body of Christ, whose head is the church (Eph 1:10); Christ's body and limbs are the church (1:23); there is a hierogamic (bride and bridegroom) relationship between Christ and his Church (5: 21–33). If, with Paul, in *totus Christus* we include Christ as head and body as his church, we are on the road toward a theological (mariological) sophiology.

Let us interpret Paul's teachings on wisdom in the first epistle to the Corinthians in this light. He says: "But we preach Christ crucified, unto the Jews indeed a stumbling block, and unto the Gentiles foolishness: But unto them that are called, both Jews and Greeks, Christ the power of God, and the wisdom of God" (1 Cor 1: 23–24) and "But of him are you in Christ Jesus, who of God is made unto us wisdom" (1 Cor 1:30).

These excerpts are significant. According to conventional interpretation they refer to the Logos as God's wisdom and the second excerpt indeed remains in this frame of mind: Christ became our wisdom. Yet, the two features, God's power and his wisdom, may be distinct as well, in which case one refers to Logos (or the Word), while the other to Sophia. Furthermore, the expression: "of him are you in Christ Jesus," alludes to Wisdom and thus all elements, Christ, his head, his body, and his brides (the Church) appear together; the Christological and the ecclesiological dimensions complement one another.

At a certain point, Paul speaks even more clearly about the ecclesiological dimension of Sophia: "As you reading, may understand my knowledge in the mystery of Christ, Which in other generations was not known to the sons of men, as it is now revealed to his holy apostles and prophets in the Spirit. . . . That the manifold wisdom of God may be made known to the principalities and powers in heavenly places through the church" (Eph 3:4–5, 10).

Therefore, the wisdom of God is revealed by the Church and embodied in the Church. The Church is the embodiment of Sophia. That Sophia and the Church stand side by side may be confirmed by the fact that both are feminine in both Latin and Greek: *Sophia*, *Ecclesia*.

In fact, the manifold, multi-shaped, and versatile character of Sophia may resonate with further representations of Sophia, the cosmic role of Hokmah and Shekinah of the Kabbalah, or even, as we have noted, the parallels with other religions and the philosophical proposition: the form of forms constitutes the basic formal principle of everything. In light of this argument, the role of Sophia for Paul is much more significant than one would have believed earlier.

Before continuing with the analysis of scripture and before we can arrive at any definitive conclusion, however, we have to follow up with the changes in how the Christian tradition treats Sophia, because over the centuries such aspects gained a prominence that will enable us to re-evaluate our theorems.

7

The Teaching of the Church Fathers on Sophia

T HE TEACHING of revelations rose to such heights in the field of sophiology that it makes one dizzy to look at these horizons. Nevertheless, we have to continue our inquiry: What sort of Christian proof can we find about Sophia? Although scattered seeds of truth regarding religious experiences of Sophia cannot be compared with the peak represented by scripture, they may be treated as testimonies of a tradition in a wider sense. First, let us have a look at the patristic age.

The Three Sophias

The most significant 5th-century representative of the Church Fathers in this field is Theodoret, bishop of Cyros, Syria. He says: "There are three Sophias: one who provides us with understanding and intellect, with the help of whom we know how to practice the arts and develop sciences, and with the help of whom we can become acquainted with God; there is another one, whom we can contemplate in creation. And there is a third one, who has revealed herself through our Redeemer, and whom the unbelievers call folly."

Taking Theodoret's conclusions into consideration, we need to differentiate between human wisdom, which is a gift of God, and theological wisdom, which is a property of God and which manifests itself in His relationship to creation, and, further, between Divine wisdom, which is related to one of the members of the Holy Trinity: either the Son of God, or the Holy Spirit.

Let us have a look at these aspects.

1. Sophia, as a human capacity, is technical, intellectual, or moral in its nature. Clement of Alexandria, following a venerable tradition even in his own time, says that philosophy is the study of wisdom. It is the study of the wisdom whose aim is to discover what is human and what is divine.[1] Saint Gregory of Nazianzen sees *"gnothi seauton"* as the consequence of Wisdom: "Wisdom means learning who we are."[2] At the same time, wisdom is the gift of God. This is the view of Nazianzen in his comment on Isaiah 11:2, where wisdom is the gift of the Spirit.

2. Wisdom also is a divine attribute or a unique property of God. As Dionysius the Areopagite says, "The divine Sophia knows everything, because she knows herself."[3]

3. In addition, Wisdom is a divine person who has a special relationship with the Holy Trinity, and who might even be identical with one of the divine persons.

(a) However surprising it might be, several followers of the early Church hold that Wisdom is identical with the Holy Spirit. Theophilos of Antioch (†186) sees the Holy Spirit in Sophia: "The Father, who reveals His Logos (*endiathetos*) concealed in Himself along with His Sophia before everything else."[4] In the first three days of creation Theophilos sees the image of the Trinity: "The image of God and His Logos and Sophia."[5] In his explanation of Genesis 1:26 he writes the following to Autolycus: "'Let us create' means that He creates with His Logos and Sophia."[6]

Irenaeus of Lyons holds a similar view. In *Adversus Haereses* he discusses the Sethianers, who call the Holy Spirit the sister or bride of Christ. He draws the following parallel: "Begetting and depiction (*Progenies et figuratio*), the Son and the Holy Spirit, or Logos and Sophia."[7] He has a similar interpretation of "Let us create" as well: "Logos and Sophia, the Son and the Holy Spirit always stand next to

---

1. *Patrologia Graeca* (PG) 8, 721 B.
2. PG 36, 200 A.
3. PG 3, 869 B.
4. PG 6, 1064 C.
5. Ibid., 6, 1077 B.
6. Ibid., 1081 B.
7. PL 7, 993 A.

Him (next to the Father), to whom He says: 'Let us create man.'"[8]
Elsewhere he says that "[The Father] made everything solid through
the Logos, and He connects everything through Sophia."[9]

Clement of Alexandria already had an interpretation of this passage and emphasized the role of Sophia as a co-creator, but it is dif-
ficult to decide whether he uses this expression for Logos or for the
Holy Spirit.[10]

(b) And now we have arrived at the patristic view, which regards
Sophia as Christ, Logos, the Son of God. This is the *logosophic*
school of thought.[11] It is a Christological interpretation of Sophia.
How widespread this view once was is indicated by the fact that
Arius used it to argue for the created nature of the Logos: Wisdom
seems to be a creature. Saint Athanasius rejected this view concerning the Logos, but he had no convincing arguments based on Scripture to prove that Sophia was not created.

Origen also assumes that Logos and Sophia are identical: "Christ
is the highest wisdom of God, our Father and the Logos."[12] Epipha-
nius likewise believes that the two are identical: "The Wisdom of the
Father is God's only Logos."[13] Sophroniscus relates Sophia to Mary
in the sense that she was also given birth by a Divine Parent, since
she is the Logos: "You alone bore in your womb the only Wisdom,
oh Divine Mother."[14]

(c) The heresy of Arius clearly shows where it leads if we regard
Wisdom only as a created force, and if we only regard what the literature of wisdom says about Sophia as a preliminary image pointing
exclusively toward Christ. There was a theological vacuum in

8. Ibid., 1032 B.

9. *Compingens*, viz. *omnia componens* in the *Vulgate*, Wis 8:30; the LXX uses the
expression *harmosousa* = harmony creator. *PL* 7, 1038 B and 967 B.

10. Clemens A., *Hom.* 16, 12.

11. This "logosophian turn" perhaps played an important role with regard to
the fear of the polytheism of the ancient religions as well as the fear of Gnosticism,
which was a serious enemy of Christianity, but was also the patriarchal comprehension of society and its hierarchy.

12. *PG* 17, 28 B.

13. *PG* 42, 296.

14. *PG* 87, 3880 A.

ancient times concerning the question of Sophia, which was filled only by the thoughts of Gnostic, hermetic, kabbalistic, and esoteric schools for a long time.

Gnosticism gave birth to rich sophiological speculation. For example, the Coptic Papyrus Berolinensis from 502 contains three 5th-century works rich in allusions to Sophia: *The Gospel according to Mary, The Apocryphal Gospel of John,* and a work called *The Sophia of Jesus Christ.*[15]

At the same time, slowly a process of reinterpretation started to take place in the Eastern Church. The famous Hagia Sophia in Constantinople, built by Emperor Justinian, had been consecrated to the Logos that became man. It reflected a Christological point of view commemorated at Christmas. The Cathedral of Saint Sophia in Kiev had been consecrated to the Divine Mother. For a while it was called the Cathedral of the Divine Parent. However, the Church of Sophia in Novgorod, whose icon is a copy of the picture of Sophia in Constantinople, had been consecrated to the celebration of the Divine Parent's fall into a slumber. (We will discuss the artistic aspects of all that later.) Gradually, a new approach was born, primarily in the Russian Church, to the interpretation of the Sophia theory during the transition from the age of the Church Fathers to the modern age.

(d) Saint Augustine is also an important Sophianic witness. He produced the most extensive literature about Sophia in ancient times. His major works on this topic are the *De Incarnatione Verbi, De Civitate Dei, De Doctrina Christiana, Confessiones,* and *Liber Meditationum.* He recognizes two types of Wisdom. One is Uncreated Wisdom, or *Sapientia Increata,* which, similarly to his forerunners, the Greek fathers, especially Origen and Athanas, he identifies with Logos: "*Sapientiam verbum Dei esse intelligendum.*"[16]

The other type is Created Wisdom, or *Sapientia Creata,* which possesses maternal features. He calls it "our mother in heaven" and "heavenly Jerusalem" in his works. He identifies Created Wisdom

---

15. Walter Till, *Die gnostischen Schriften des Papyrus Berolensis* (Berlin: Uhlstein, 1955), 96.

16. "We should regard wisdom as the word of God," *De Incarnatione, PL* 42, 1178.

mainly with the church. See one of his prayers: "O domus luminosa et speciosa." This theological approach was further developed by St. Bonaventure, Nicholas of Cusa, and St. Hildegard of Bingen.

Sometimes it is nearly impossible to decide which aspect of Divine Wisdom Augustine is discussing. He is definitely familiar with the cosmic figure of Sophia from the books of wisdom and Greek philosophy. In his interpretation, the passage "there is spirit inside of her" (Wisdom 7:22) means that the ideas or *rationes seminales*[17] of things are hidden inside of her. In his view, God creates the world looking at these ideas, and based on that he could have even interpreted it as uncreated.

He goes even further in his commentary on Genesis. In Genesis 1:1, for example, he interprets the *boe-resit*, the *en-arche* as *in* Wisdom and *with* Wisdom God created heaven and earth.[18] If we apply this translation to John 1:1, assuming that Sophia and Logos are identical, we will reach the impossible conclusion that "Logos was in Logos." It makes a lot more sense to treat the two as two separate ideas: Logos was in Sophia. Considering all of the above, it is by no means certain that Augustine actually held that Logos = Sophia.

The most probable explanation is that Augustine places Sophia at the utmost end of created being. That is how she can become the beholder, carrier, and most important idea of all the other creatures. That is why he decorates her with such attributes as *"particeps aeternitatis Dei"* (part of the eternity of God),[19] and *"creatura creaturarum maxima"* (the highest of all creatures).[20] The relationship between *Sapientia Creata* and *Increata* is the same as the relationship between *"lumen illuminans et lumen illuminatum"* (enlightening light and enlightened light).[21]

It is the parallel of light, the theory of illumination that makes it clear that Augustine treats Created Wisdom as an intelligent being, a person: *"Sapientia creata est spiritualis naturae quae contemplatione*

17. *Civitas Dei* XI 10, 3.
18. *Confessiones* XX, *PL* 32, 836/29.
19. Ibid. XIII, *PL* 32, 16.
20. *Liber medit.* XIX, *PL* 40, 916.
21. Ibid., 915.

luminis lumen est" (Created Wisdom is spiritual in nature, and through the contemplation of light it is light itself).[22] Here he openly declares: "*Sapientia creata: mens rationalis et intellectualis*" (Created Wisdom: a rational and intelligent soul), who is "*Idonea faciem Dei semper videre*" (always ready to contemplate the face of God), similarly to how the angels act according to Christ (Matt 18:10).

Augustine holds that this cosmic Sophia who unites the created world is nothing other than the Soul of the World: "*Mens pura, concordissime una*"[23] (the only Soul that unites everything = Soul of the World), which connects us to heaven. This Sophia/World Soul is definitely feminine and maternal in nature: "*Mater nostra, Jerusalem quae sursum est et libera*" (Our Mother, Jerusalem, who is up above and free) says Augustine following St. Paul.[24] And now the road is open to a mariological and ecclesiological interpretation exercised by such people as Hildegard of Bingen, Jakob Boehme, Vladimir Solovyov, Pavel Florensky, and others.

22. Ibid.
23. Ibid., 916.
24. (The free woman) means the heavenly Jerusalem. She is our mother (Gal 4:26).

8

The Confession
of the Eastern Church

Sophia in Greek Liturgy[1]

I GREW UP with a liturgical tradition in Greek Catholicism that follows the practices of the Eastern Church. Our liturgy, even in its simplified form, is full of allusions to Divine Wisdom. In the Liturgy of St. John Chrysostom, as in many other practices of worship that make use of a reading from scripture, the exclamation "Wisdom!" is uttered on numerous occasions. The invocation "Wisdom! [Sophia (*Premudrosty* in Church Slavonic)] (or Wisdom), let us be attentive!" is uttered every time a reading from scripture is to follow.[2]

According to conventional interpretation, here Sophia signifies divine Logos. She is also identical in the line cited at Easter: "Most sacred Pasch, Christ, oh Wisdom, Word of God and Fortification."[3] The liturgy also reminds us of the nuptial structure of being when the Word of God is personified as bridegroom: "Let us appear in front of Christ resurrected with burning candles as if in front of the bridegroom of the wedding ceremony."[4] Therefore, one should match Logos with its polar pair, Sophia, who is addressed in the

---

1. Viz. Cselényi, "Az Isteni Bölcsesség a keleti egyházban és az orosz vallás-bölcseletben" ["Divine Wisdom in the Eastern Church and in Russian Philosophy of Religion"] in *Új Sion* [*New Sion*] I (XLIII) 2007/2: 171–87.

2. A puzzling parallel: the prefix 'pre' in *Premudrosty* is the same amplification as the prefix 'pra' in the Buddhist expression, *Pragnya*; both means 'very much' or 'excessively' and thus Premudrosty means 'outstanding' or greatest wisdom.

3. *The Easter Canon of Saint John of Damascus*, "Ode IX: trope 2."

4. Ibid. "Ode V: trope 3."

Akathist Hymn as follows: "Hail, divine spouse!"[5] Furthermore, this is exactly the form in which one of the chants of the vespers addresses Sophia. Therefore, the Eastern liturgy opens the way to a view of Sophia as the carrier of the feminine features of God.

The figure of Sophia usually appears in a mariological dimension in the Eastern liturgy. In Byzantine chant, the mother of God is often connected to wisdom: "Celebrating the most sacred and most blessed feast of the heavenly wise mother of God today, come to worship and applaud so that we glorify God born from her."[6] Likewise, "She is the storehouse of the wisdom of God,"[7] and "She is the ray of the Sun of intellect, a lightning illuminating our soul."[8]

It looks as if the tradition of the Kabbalah and wisdom literature could survive in Eastern liturgy: Mary is often depicted as Jerusalem and Sion or heavenly Jerusalem following the depiction in the Book of Revelation. Additionally, one of the most beautiful Easter chants captures the sentiment: "Shine, shine heavenly Jerusalem for the glorious light of the Lord has come; rejoice and revel new Sion and you, Mother of God, rejoice in the resurrection of your son."

To describe the status of a mother bearing God, Eastern tradition uses a number of Sophia-symbols: "You are the throne of the king of heaven,"[9] "food sweeter than manna, a land of milk and honey,"[10] "vessel of divine embodiment,"[11] "abode of the Lord, a shaded hill, a golden sconce, the garden of paradise, divine table, tent, a golden door-handle,"[12] "the gates of heaven, light illuminating the entire world,"[13] "the purest abode of our Redeemer, rich palace, the sacred treasury of divine glory, the angels sing of you: You are the palace of

---

5. Tone 7, vespers for Saturday, chant of the sticheron and prelude for Mother of God.
6. *Katavasia of the Mother of God*, "Ode VI."
7. *Hymn of Akathistos*, strophe 9, verse 1.
8. Ibid., strophe 11, trope 2.
9. Ibid., strophe 1, trope 3.
10. Ibid., strophe 6, trope 3.
11. Ibid., trope 4.
12. *Paraklis*, closing verse of sticheron and prelude.
13. Ibid., 2nd sticheron and prelude.

heaven,"[14] "we name you palace and its door, burning royal chair, untouched mountain, non-inflammable briar."[15] These *epiteton ornans* remind us of the concept of Shekinah.

Eastern liturgy endows Mary with cosmic attributes that make her seem identical with Sophia: "Every creature, the order of angels and all of humankind rejoices in you. You are the blessed shelter, spiritual Garden of Eden, your womb became the heavenly throne and your inner being is more eloquent than the heaven."[16] Mary is placed above the angels by the liturgy, at the highest rank of created beings: "You are esteemed more than the cherubim and incomparably more glorified than the seraphim." The Eastern liturgy also reminds us that the cosmic Sophia (*Hokmah*) "is initiated into mysterious schemes,"[17] and is a forerunner in alluding to the principle of Cusa, his *coincidentia oppositorum*, and applies it to Sophia-Mary, "who smoothed oppositions."[18]

The liturgy presents an intimate relationship between Mary-Sophia and the Holy Trinity: "by whom the secret of the Holy Trinity was revealed," and her relationship to the Father and the Word is also expressed: "The tent of God and the Word."[19] Often allusions are made to *hieros gamos,* to which Sophia is part. "You were marked by the Holy Spirit as the fiancée of God and the Father," claims a liturgical chant.[20] In another place she is the divine spouse.[21] Another aspect of the holy nuptial is also known by the East: the Virgin "is the bride of Christ, the king of the universe."[22] Here what appears, then, is the relationship of Logos and the cosmic Sophia and Mary is the carrier of this role.

---

14. November 21, Feast of the Presentation of Mary to the Temple, kontakion.
15. *Akathistos*, Strophe 1, verse 3.
16. *The liturgy of Saint Basil the Great.*
17. *Akathistos*, strophe 2, verse 2.
18. Ibid., strophe 8, trope 2.
19. *Akathistos*, strophe 12, trope 1.
20. November 21 (feast of introducing Mary to the church) lauds, 3rd sticheron.
21. Tone 7, vespers for Saturday, chant of the sticheron and prelude for Mother of God.
22. November 21, 2nd vespers.

Furthermore, she is also bonded to the Holy Spirit: "She is introduced today in the house of the Lord, bringing the inspiration of the Holy Spirit."[23] "She is the tabernacle gilded by the Holy Spirit."[24] The expression that the Virgin as the fiancée of the Holy Spirit only appears in popular songs in the East; in the liturgy she is rather the projection of the work of the Holy Spirit and the radiation of its presence.

This liturgy, common prayer, and hymnody, shaped between the middle and the end of the first millennium, is a vivid testimony of the lively presence of the Sophia of scripture, and they form the basis of the veneration of Mary in the second millennium and, indirectly, to Palamitism and especially to Russian sophiology.

The Palamite Mariology

It is not only the sporadic presence of the Sophia concept in the Eastern Church that helps preserve the tradition of sophiology, but it also spreads the veneration of Mary.

As we have seen, Patristics places Sophia on the borderline of created and non-created being and leaves open the possibility of seeking the maternal principle in God; and has intimated that we could see the Virgin mother as the primary embodiment of Sophia. The theology of the Eastern Church carried on with this tradition from the beginning of the second millennium, specifying former findings of sophiology within mariology. The strongest theological trend in this regard within the Orthodox Church was Palamitism.

Palamitism is the 14th-century synthesis of Orthodox theology that extended Byzantine theological traditions in Christology and mariology. Four great authors have to be mentioned here: the founder of the school of thought, Saint Gregory of Palamas (c. 1296–1359), who was archbishop of Thessalonike from 1347; Nikolaos Kabasilas, an unordained theologian, who was born around 1320 and died after 1396; Theophanes, archbishop of Nicaea, who died in

---

23. November 21, kontakion.
24. *Akathistos*, strophe 5, trope 2.

1381; and Isidoros Glabas, who was also archbishop of Thessalonike and died in 1397.

The theology of Palamitism is quite well known. A real distinction (*distinctio realis*) is supposed to exist between the essence of God and His activity (*energeia*); the energies are considered noncreated mercies and the essence of salvation is not seen in the recognition of the divine essence, but, rather, in the substantiation, in having a share in divine attributes what may occur with the help of divine energies. In this theology, the God-bearing Virgin (the Theotokos), holds a special place.

Gregory of Palamas sees a mediating role of the Virgin Mary in the fact that she, being the Mother of God, is the connecting bond between God and His creatures. Since she gave birth to God the Creator, she became queen of all creatures in heaven and on earth.[25] Gregory names Mary *Kyria* (Lady) who reigns over everything.[26] He applies the expression of Psalm 45, ("sitting on the right of the Messiah") to Mary and, further, on the basis of Isaiah and Ezekiel, he sees her as the throne itself (Isaiah 6:1; Ezekiel 1:3 and 12).[27]

Based on one of the teachings of Eastern theology, namely, that "God took a human form in order that man could become divine," Saint Gregory of Palamas claims that Mary, by giving birth to God for man, formed God into a human being since, according to the relation of similarities (viz. Gen 1:26), the changes are only valid mutually: God became similar to us.[28] On the other hand, however, man's divinization[29] makes every one of us sons of God. God descended to earth through the mediation of Mary, and we are meant to ascend to heaven through her.[30] The idea is extraordinary.

On the question of Mary's mediation, Mary's virginity is fundamental for Gregory. She conceived and bore her holy Son "with no seed," without the interaction of man:[31] this alone marks how spe-

25. *Patrologia Graeca* (PG) 151, 465 [B].
26. *PG* 151, 172 [A].
27. Ibid., 172 [B].
28. Ibid., 465 [B].
29. *Homiliae Gregorii Palamae* (Athenis: Gregorios, 1861) (hereafter *Pal.*), 137.
30. *Pal.*, 138.
31. *Pal.*, 123–25.

cial a relationship binds her to the persons of the Holy Trinity. She bore in her soul all of the Holy Trinity.[32] Thus, we have to recognize that no one loved God as much as did Mary, and God (the Son of God) loved no one as much as He loved Mary, since He chose her as His mother before the beginning of time.

Mary's virginal motherhood underscores the fact that he whom she gave birth to as a virgin in body is the same person who was born by the Father virginally and eternally.[33] In the Byzantine Rite, the idea is expressed in a Christmas sticheron: Christ "was born eternally without a mother and was born into time by a mother without a father." Mary as the virgin mother, therefore, solidifies the relationship between man and God, and her role as a unique mediator is confirmed.

From the aspect of an ecumenical dialogue with Protestantism, what Gregory has to say on Mary and her relation to redemption may become significant. Although he does not go so far as coining the term "immaculate conception"—that is, conception without original sin, which is a more recent idea even in Catholic theology[34]—and in fact claims that only God is free of sin, and, therefore, only the conception of Christ could have happened without sin, Gregory points out that Mary's chosen role as the mother of the Redeemer necessitates that God had made her originally immaculate.[35] She is immaculate not independently of Christ; rather, she is so by her intimate relationship with Christ and for his sake.

Gregory uses several such images and expressions. Mary is more than a saint; she is the summit and totality of all holiness; she is the mother of goodness and receiver of all gifts of mercy because she could bear the one who possessed all treasures (viz. Col 2:3); she is the saint of saints,[36] the innermost shrine where only the chief priest could enter (viz. Heb 6:20), the receiver of the Immeasurable, the borderline between created and non-created,[37] the altar of heav-

---

32. *Pal.*, 160.
33. *Pal.*, 10, 12, 127.
34. See Denz. 1641.
35. *Pal.*, 123.
36. *Pal.*, 145–46.
37. *Pal.*, 151, 177[A-B].

enly bread, a living tabernacle not created by human hand, the soil of the eternal plantation. We have met some of these images in the texts of the Byzantine liturgy. Each of the above terms suggests that the mother of God is the connecting tie between the spheres of the divine and the human, not by herself, but by the role in which she guides us to Christ, to God in man.

Although Gregory does not apply the term "New Eve" to Mary, yet, from the context, it is obvious this is what he believes. Mary freed us from Eve's malediction,[38] she bore Christ without pain, and the angelic *Ave* absolved us from penitence for the sin of Adam and Eve. Her special connection to redemption is confirmed by the fact that she shared the fate of the Redeemer in the most profound way: she escorted and guided her holy Son in His life, in His suffering and death, and in His resurrection and glorification.

Concerning resurrection, Gregory advocates the concept originally of Syrian background according to which the resurrected Christ first appeared in front of Mary; they see "the other Mary" of Matthew 27:61 as the Holy Virgin and, since at Pentecost Mary is with the Apostles, Gregory supposes that after the glorification of Christ she assisted and counselled the heralds of the gospel, that is the proto-Church.[39] Ultimately, what he says is that Mary is the Mother of the Church.

Given such representations of Mary, Gregory arrives at a new mediating role for the mother of God. Bernardus Schulze sums up Gregory's train of thought in saying that one can claim that Mary is our mediator because she is the mother of God and thereby she connects humankind to God.[40] As the mother of the Creator, she became the queen of every creature, for all of which she cares. Since she is the mother of all possible mercy, holiness, and light, she radiates mercy, holiness, and light to men and angels alike. The root of her mediation is her love toward God and God's love toward her and every one of us.

---

38. *PG* 151, 172[Cs].
39. Ibid., 464[Bs].
40. Bernard Schulze, "Theologi palamitae saec. XIV de mediatione Mariae," in *De mariologia et oecumenismo* (Roma: Città Nuova, 1962), 355.

Gregory claims that Mary is both the catalyst between man and God in the order of being *and* our mediator in the moral order; that is, she helps those who turn to her. He holds that Mary is a mediator not only for men but also for angels, because the Son, who performed the task of redemption, appeared through her exclusively. Schulze believes that Gregory borrowed the idea from Dionysius when he claims that Mary is a universal mediator both existentially and morally.

These principles of Palamite theology may sound alien to Protestants, who believe in the exclusive mediating role of Christ (viz. 1 Timothy 2:5). However, Palamite mariology merely attempts to guide seeking souls to Christ and, as Schulze points out, these mariological principles become reasonable only if we keep in mind the intimate, ontological relationship of the Son to His Holy Mother. Within this loving relationship jealousy, discord, and conflict are impossible. The historical fact that Mary is chosen and elevated *by* the Holy Trinity to the rank and honor of becoming the mother of God (and of every one of us) is sufficiently clear from scripture.

Further Along the Road of Palamitism

Nikolaos Kabasilas surpasses Palamite mariology in his treatment of the privileges of the Holy Mother of God. He argues that Mary could have only been the abode of the most Holy (i.e., Jesus), the golden vessel holding the manna, Aaron's seeds, and the plates of the Covenant, if her soul was immaculate.[41] In other words, Kabasilas recognizes that the Holy Mother of God must have been without any sin even before the blessings of the angels. Scholars do not agree whether this means being free of original sin, Mary's immaculate conception, and thus a kind of *praeredemptio* or redemption before the time of Christ. However, for Kabasilas, Mary is the carrier of a cleansed human nature.[42] At the same time, he holds that this privilege of Mary foreshadows Christ who, as the "great chief priest," will step into the innermost sanctuary.

41. *PG* XIX, 477, 32–38.
42. *PG* 491, 34.

Theophanes of Nicaea adds new colors to this mariology. Based on Dionysius the Areopagite, St. Maximus the Confessor, and St. John of Damascus, he sees that the single person alluded to in Ephesians 1:10 is Mary.[43] The proof of this supposition for him is the embodiment in which God embraced and unified within Himself the whole of human nature and this happened through the Holy Mother of God. At the same time, he believes that the ultimate ascension of man must also occur through Mary: she is going to be the mediator in our divinization.[44]

But Theophanes goes one step further. Since man, as a microcosm, bears the entire created world within him, Mary's role as mediator must be extended to the whole world. He recognizes that the only access to the Father is through the Son; but, likewise, we can only reach the Son through the Mother of God, and this is why Mary is the mediator not only of man but also of the angels in the process of becoming divine. He expresses this conviction by calling Mary heaven (viz. in the canon of Easter Mary is the heavenly Jerusalem).[45] These features of Mary are, in many respects, in parallel with the cosmic and eschatological dimensions of Sophia.

Isidoros Glabas, following the ideas of Theophanes, concludes that the expression, "he that is mighty hath done to me great things" (Luke 1:49) proves that Mary was free from sin, and the verse of Psalm 51:5, "in sin did my mother conceive me" does not apply to her. The divine image of man is realized in Mary; she best resembles God and God became like us through her. This aspect, again, demonstrates Mary's role as mediator: we became similar to God through her. Isidoros names Mary "salvation" in his last mariological homily[46] (viz. "our salvation" in *paraklis*) in the sense that Mary is the first to reach salvation and thus she becomes a model for our salvation.

According to Schulze, these theorems, perhaps surprising to our ears, are based on Mary's Holy motherhood of God.[47] In His

43. Nicaenus, *Sermo in Sanctissimam Deiparam*, ed. M. Jugie (Letouzey et Ane: Paris, 1933), 356.
44. Ibid., 54.
45. Ibid., 46.
46. Ibid., 164 [C].
47. Schulze, *Palamitae*, 418.

humanity only can she be said to have borne God (the Son). The Son became visible through her mediation and could only perform the task of redemption through her. In the view of Palamite theologians, the fact of embodiment binds Mary to Christ, the Redeemer, in a unique relationship; but also binds her to the Father and to the Holy Spirit, which is a clear sign of God's philanthropic love toward man.

According to the Creed, God was embodied by Mary. Palamitism sees this in a reciprocal argument: God became man by Mary, but man also attained a chance to become a part of divine nature by Mary. This is why we can say that Mary foreshadows salvation; she is the first to be granted salvation and thus the mediator of salvation toward man. However, the idea of mediation becomes reasonable only with Christ. The way to salvation, according to Palamite thinking, is through Mary to Christ and through Christ to the Father. In the fact of Mary's mediation this ontological relationship becomes an existential and moral experience.

Palamite thinking, similarly to the ideas of sophiology, places Mary on the borderline of the created and non-created existential order; it regards her as the first fruit of divination and they believe that divine attributes are reflected in her. Many scholars see these aspects of Palamitism as a proof of the Protestant accusation, which argues that Catholicism deifies Mary, or the criticism of Jung, who disapproves of Mary being seen as complementary with the Holy Trinity in a divine quaternary. Far from it: Mary is not a goddess in Palamitism. In Palamite theology deification is the ultimate objective of every one of us and this deification would not mean attaining the essence of the divine, but only the possession of divine energies and of non-created mercy. According to Palamite thought, the Holy Mother of God is *only* the recipient of glory through mercy.

9

Sophia in the
Western Tradition

Representations of Sophia in the Early Middle Ages

THE IDEA that the Latin Church of the Middle Ages was not concerned with Sophia is false. Indeed, a number of documents and works of art from this period clearly reflect the presence of a sophianic sensibility. They may be few in number, but they are rather impressive.

We can find a number of illustrations of Sophia in biblical codices and manuscripts. The best known of such illustrations is from the *Codex Rossanus*, produced in the 6th century in Rossano (Calabria) in the south of Italy. It depicts Mark the evangelist with a roll of the Gospel in his hand. He is inspired not by the muses, but by Sophia. His clothes are blue, the color of Sophia.[1]

Four figures are depicted in the miniature of *Codex Syriacus* (6th–7th c.)[2] depicting Sophia, King Solomon, and Mary with her child under her heart. On Sophia's shoulder there is a cross, and on her arm as well as on the arm of Solomon there is a book (The Book of Wisdom). Its Christological meaning is that Solomon and the literature of wisdom are the prefiguration of Christ, who is incarnated through Mary. According to the sophiological interpretation, Sophia is the prefiguration of Mary, and Solomon is the prefigura-

---

1. Franz Lilienfeld, "Frau Weisheit in byzantinischen und karolingischen Quellen," in *Typos, Symbol und Allegorie bei den östlichen Vätern und ihren Parallellen* (Eischtaerr: Internationales Kolloquium 1981), 156, 160.
2. Held in the Bibliothèque nationale, Paris. See appendix I.

tion of the Son of God. Lilienfeld holds that it would be tautological to view both the figure of Solomon and of Sophia as the preliminary image of the Logos.[3]

The approach according to which Solomon is the preliminary image of the Son of God seems to be justified, since scripture calls David the Son of God (Samuel 7:14).[4] Such an idea is not without historical precedent: in Egypt the king was regarded as the son of the god Ra, whereas the Sumerians and Babylonians regarded their king as the adopted child of God. Solomon is also called "Jedidiah" in scripture, which means "the favorite of God" (Samuel 12:25). In an interesting parallel, (according to Proverbs 8:30), Sophia is "Amon Yahweh," or the beloved one, the love and bride of God. In the same way as Solomon is the prefiguration of the Logos and Christ, Sophia is the prefiguration of Mary (the Wisdom that became flesh).[5]

Solomon and Sophia are almost like bridegroom and bride in a *hieros gamos* relationship, similar to the bride/bridegroom relationship in the Book of Wisdom (8:2 and 8:9), where the *hieros gamos* and marriage of Logos and Sophia are foreshadowed. This dual phenomenon is further emphasized by the cross, as it is the classical symbol of polarity: it connects heaven and earth, directions and hearts. The shadow of the cross indicates that incarnation is a kenosis for both the Son of God and Sophia, who shows man the light and helps him become part of the Divine.

It is rather uncommon to depict Sophia carrying a cross, which suggests that she shares the suffering that is part of the history of the Logos. Like the incarnated Sophia, the Holy Virgin carries her child in her lap. Therefore, this early Christian miniature from Syria is a special example of Mary's sophiological dimensions. It shows Sophia as the pre-existence of Mary. She is the bride of the Logos, whose incarnation is Mary, and she is also the mother and workmate of the incarnate Logos.

3. Lilienfeld, "Frau Weisheit," 159.
4. Michael Lurkerm, *Wörterbuch Biblischer Bilder und Symbole* (München: Barth, 1973), 294.
5. Schipflinger, *Sophia*, 72.

Sophia in the High Middle Ages

The next witness is a miniature from the 12th century. It is a Hagia Sophia depiction[6] in the Stammheim Missal.[7] The Logos is above in the middle. Underneath, as indicated by a sign, stands *Sapientia*, Sophia. The meaning is obvious: she is the female creator of the world (a co-creator). There is a sign on her scapular: "I have created the world with her" (Proverbs 8:22). She is holding the half-length portrait up high, suggesting that she is the one who conceived, bore, and gave birth to the Logos and she is the one who gives the Logos to man. She is, then, the path that leads man and the world to the Logos and to God. The other figures of the miniature are saints of the Old Testament (Abraham, David, Isaac, and Zachariah). They are the ones who carried *Sapientia* and gave her to us. Two of the saints of the New Testament (John and Matthew) are also present: they represent the new people of the incarnated Logos. Consequently, the German Catholic Middle Ages had several witnesses of Sophia. These witnesses are the missing links.

The next witness is St. Hildegard of Bingen, a Benedictine abbess, who lived between 1098 and 1179. Her most important works concerning Sophia are *Scivias* (*Know the Ways*), *Liber divinorum operum* (*The Book of the Works of God*, hereafter *LDO*), and *Liber vitae meritorum* (*The Book of the Merits of Life*). Her writings were illustrated by wonderful panel paintings, most of them depicting the visions of Hildegard. We can capture her thoughts with the help of these images and their explanations. The Sophia visions of Hildegard fall into three main categories. The first is of *Hokma Yahweh*, the Sophia of God, contributor to creation, the mother and soul of the world. Another is of Sophia-Mary of the New Testament, the bride of God and mother of the Church. The third is most surprising: here she identifies Sophia with the Holy Spirit. But let us proceed step by step.

---

6. Appendix II.

7. Adam Boeckler, *Deutsche Buchmalerei in vorgotischer Zeit* (Königstein: König, 1953), 53.

Hildegard refers to Sophia as "the Queen of Virtues" (3rd Vision, the human Sophia) and as "Thora" (10th vision), but her 2nd vision is even more important in this respect.[8] Its illustration[9] depicts a woman whose womb is a giant circle with a man standing inside. The figure of the woman is crowned with another head. The mother figure is Sophia, or *Hakmoth Yahweh*.[10] She stands below Yahweh, who is symbolized by a male head; she is his descendant. She upholds and carries the universe. She is the mother and co-creator of the world, subordinated to Yahweh (Wisdom 8:1). In the center of her womb (which represents the universe) stands a man. He is the incarnate Son of God radiating light and strength in all directions. It is clear that Sophia has a cosmic role and possesses maternal features. She is one with the universe. She is at the top of the hierarchy of all created things. The center, the goal, and the meaning of her entire being, is He who is the center of the universe and redeemer of the world: Christ.

There are three figures in the 1st illustration[11] of her 9th vision. On the left is Mary; on the right is Wisdom (in the form of a woman) writing her books. Between them stands the figure of a seraph. The Virgin, decorated with gems, implies that Sophia is the representation of all the beauty of the world and Mary is the embodiment of Wisdom.[12]

The central figure is the seraph. The Sophia icons of the Eastern Church often depict Wisdom as a seraph or angel. The source is probably Wisdom 7:26, according to which Wisdom is "a spirit who is intelligent and holy." Without paying attention to the details, it is primarily a bird figure, which is unmistakably the representation of the Holy Spirit, who hovered above the waters (Gen 1:2) and descended in the form of a dove (Matt 3:16). It is depicted with six seraph wings, which represent the efficacy of the Spirit of love. (According to Romans 8:26, the spirit sighs within us when we

8. *LDO* 48.
9. Appendix III.
10. *Hakmoth* is the plural of *Hokmah*.
11. Appendix IV.
12. *LDO* 280.

pray.) The seraph is covered with scales, a reference to Holy Water: we have to be born again from water and the Holy Spirit (John 3:5).

In order to have a better understanding of Hildegard's wonderful images, we should take a look at the fish and bird symbolism of different religions. In Semitic culture, for example, the dove is the symbolic animal of Ishtar, the goddess of love, life, and fertility. The goose is the symbolic animal of Aphrodite. Hildegard says the following about the picture: "The body of the fish refers to the hidden nature of the fish, the origin and ways of which are unknown." Here she refers to the words of Jesus: "The wind blows where it wishes and you hear the sound of it, but do not know where it comes from and where it is going" (John 3:8).

The symbolism of water and the Sun is linked to that of the fish. Water is the symbol of life; therefore, Wisdom is the water of life. The seraph in the picture has the head of a lion, a reference to the strength of the Holy Spirit, which, according to Wisdom 7:26, is the "reflection of the strength of God." The lion also symbolizes the Sun, which gives us heat and light and radiates life along with the water. The body of the seraph is that of a mother, carrying a grey head in her womb (as in the Greek Theotokos icons, where the Logos is represented with the wise face of an adult). It is the Holy Spirit presenting us with the Pleroma, with totality, with Christ.

Every symbol in the picture reflects the life-giving, invigorating, love-giving strength and mercy of the Holy Spirit. Based on the picture, Sophia is the perfect image and reflection of the Holy Spirit. She is a World-Spirit, but she is also responsible for our rebirth and our becoming part of the Divine; she inspires the books of the Old Testament. She is Israel, and Mary is her embodiment, the human image of the Holy Spirit, its icon, the mother and representation of the Church.[13] Indeed, Hildegard's is one of the most significant depictions of Sophia. It is an indication of the maternal nature of the Holy Spirit, and that its realization points toward Mary.

But perhaps even more significant is the illustration of Hilde-

13. Schipflinger, *Sophia*, 81.

gard's first vision:[14] Sophia and the Lamb of God.[15] Sophia, as usual, "wears" the face of the Father on her head. She appears in the form of a woman, but with the wings of an angel. The lamb with the cross is the Lamb of God, Jesus Christ, the Word that has become man. It is obvious that Sophia cannot be the Logos, since she is the one who bears the Son and gives birth to Him. This, however, implies that she is the representation of the Holy Spirit. Since the Son was born of Mary, Sophia also personifies the role of Mary. Sophia-Mary steps on the serpent, who is the devil: her son frees mankind from their sins, and, as a result, Mary-Sophia becomes the center of the universe again. As in the beginning, she is the one who constitutes its heart and soul.

The visions of Hildegard are connected through the theme of love, which is the highest of all virtues (1 Cor 13:13) and which is represented by the Hokmah-Sophia-Wisdom (Sirach 24:18: the "mother of beautiful love"). The connection between Wisdom and the Holy Spirit is apparent: the Holy Spirit is the Spirit of Love, the binding love between the Father and the Son, and Sophia is the reflection of the Holy Spirit, which projects the figure of Sophia onto the universe, the Spirit of the World, Israel, Mary, and the Church.

Several themes of the *hieros gamos* appear in Hildegard's works: Sophia is the love of Yahweh and the mother of Christ, but she is also the Church, whose head (and bridegroom) is Christ. In Hildegard's 4th vision[16] Christ appears on a throne, giving blessings with his right hand and holding the Gospels under his left arm. His throne is held by the Sophia-Church, arrayed in gold. Here we can see the virgin-like purity and readiness of the Sophia-Mary-Church to assume her motherhood and thereby further the salvation of mankind.

The influence of Hildegard is clearly present in an illustration from 1400, *The Partner of Yahweh on the Throne*, now held in the Royal Library in Belgium.[17] In the illustration, Sophia wears a purple gown and has a crown upon her head. She holds a rod in her left

14. Appendix V.
15. *LDO* 32.
16. *Scivias* 161.
17. Appendix VI.

hand and a scroll in her right hand bearing a quotation *Ab initio et ante saecula creata sum*, "I was created from the beginning before all ages" (Prov 8:23). The picture is the representation of Wisdom 8: 22–31 and Proverbs 8:3 and 9:4, where Wisdom is the lover and partner of Yahweh in creation. She is his partner on the throne and shares in his reign.

Sophia is also present in the religious art of the Renaissance. Jan van Eyck's fresco on the high altar in Ghent, painted in 1432, is one of the greatest masterpieces of Flemish art of the 15th century.[18] The fresco[19] consists of two parts: above the middle there is the Father (or Christ as king) with Mary on one side and John the Baptist on the other. At the bottom is represented the worship of the Lamb of God. In the halo above Mary there is a sign: "For she [Wisdom] is fairer than the sun and surpasses every constellation of the stars. Compared to light, she is found more radiant" (Wisdom 7:29). In other words, Mary is the representation and embodiment of wisdom.

The artist puts on canvas not only the worship of *Agnus Dei*, but the "marriage of the lamb" as well, which was announced by John the Baptist (John 3:28–29) and which is described in more detail in the Book of Revelation: "For the wedding day of the Lamb has come, his bride has made herself ready" (Rev 19:7b). The fresco depicts the Father preparing the wedding of His Son and His bride, Sophia. John the Baptist points at this secret with his finger. The figures playing music refer to the friends of the bride (Psalm 42) and the parable of the wise virgins (Matt 25:6). They also refer to Adam and Eve, who are the prototype of the *hieros gamos*.

In the middle of the lower section there is a well in the garden in front of the throne of the Lamb, a symbol of Mary and the life-giving womb of the Church. It is also the symbol of rebirth "from water and the Holy Spirit." The Holy Spirit is Mother-*Ruah*, or Mother-Spirit, who appears in the form of a dove at the top of the lower picture in the middle, radiating her rays of mercy on the entire garden. The grail, the spring, and the garden are maternal symbols as well.

---

18. *Grosses Lexikon der Malerei* (Braunschweug: Herz, 1982), 204.
19. Appendix VII.

We should also take into consideration the other symbolic names of Mary: *Vas spirituale* = the grail of the Holy Spirit; *fons signatus* = singular spring; and *hortus conclusus* = the enclosed garden, which Matthias Grünewald depicts in the Nativity in the Isenheim altarpiece (discussed below). There is a further parallel between the theologies of John and Paul. As John talks about the marriage of the Lamb of God and his bride, Sophia, in Revelation, Paul talks about the relationship between Christ and his bride, the Church (Eph 5).

The high altar of Ghent is a fascinating vision of completeness. It starts out from the pre-existent Sophia whom the Father had chosen to become the bride for His Son and whom He presented to the Son as a gift. Sophia was incarnate in Mary, who made it possible for the Son to become man, and who takes part in His saving and redeeming work (this is what John the Baptist points to as well). The final goal is the marriage of the Logos-Lamb and Sophia in heaven: the altar = throne of the Lamb in the garden is surrounded by an army of celebrating and rejoicing saints.

The High Renaissance

The most famous witness of Sophia from the beginning of the Renaissance is Michelangelo Buonarroti whose best known works are in St. Peter's Basilica, the Pietà, and the Sistine Chapel. His famous fresco *The Creation of Adam*[20] can be seen at the back of the chapel. If we take a closer look at it, we will find that there is a curious woman appearing from the cloak of the Father. Some hold that this woman is Eve. However, she cannot be Eve. She can only be Sophia, the co-creator. Therefore, the famous painting is a Sophia picture. But how could Michelangelo have arrived at this representation of Sophia?

Michelangelo lived in Florence from 1475 to 1564, where he became acquainted not only with the artistic traditions of Florence, but with the ideas of Hellenism and Platonism as well. We know that Plato linked his theories with the doctrine of the idea of ideas, which his Christian followers identified with the Hokma-Sophia

20. Appendix VIII.

figure of the Old Testament. The Accademia Platonica of Florence was founded by Marsilio Ficino (1433–1499), who tried to integrate Platonist-Neo-Platonist philosophy with Christian philosophy.[21] Ficino borrowed the Platonist idea of a World Soul and applied it to Sophia. He was the one who encouraged the creation of the altar of Isenheim as well (see below).

This is what Michelangelo represents in his famous fresco. The inquisitive face of a woman cannot be Eve not only because, according to Genesis, she was created later from Adam's rib. There is a more profound reason as well: according to the wisdom literature, God first created Sophia. Therefore, she is the *arche* or ancestress of all other creatures, the partner of God in creation. He creates the world together with her. She is the love of Yahweh. She is His partner on the throne who sees His plans and designs and gives Him advice in His work.

Adam is represented in the picture as the highest point, the crown of creation. Sophia is the woman showing interest in the creation of man and ready to choose this particular solution from Yahweh's designs. Adam will be the partner of Eve. He will be her love and treasure. He will be the prefiguration of the Logos. The self-addressing monologue of God described in Genesis 1:26–27 ("Let us create...") is, therefore, a dialogue between the Father and Sophia, with whom he shares His knowledge and being and who provides Him with advice, as described in Proverbs 8:22–23.

The next witness is the representation of Sophia-Maria on the altar of Isenheim, painted by Matthias Grünewald between 1512 and 1516.[22] Among the wonderful pictures on the tabernacle we see on the left side of the middle panel the so-called church, chapel, or tabernacle picture of Mary.[23] It compels us to believe that what we see are frames integrating different events in the history of religion. In one of these frames the Son is kneeling before the Father and praying to become a man with the help of the Holy Virgin, who is stand-

---

21. Wolfgan Dreiss, *Die Mystik des Marsilio Ficino Gross* (Berlin: 1929), 68.
22. Georg Scheja, *Der Isenheimer Altar des Matthias Grünewald* (Köln: DuMont Schauberg, 1969), 65.
23. Appendix IX.

ing ready below like a Little Madonna. In the upper part of the picture (in the blue circle of light) we can see Sophia-Mary, who is the partner of God in creation (Prov 8:22), the progenitress of creation (Wisdom 8:1), the World Soul (Wisdom 7:22–27). But the same Sophia also appears below in the form of a four-winged angel, representing the Sophia who is ready to become human in Mary and give birth to the son of God, helping him in his redeeming and saving work.

Below we can see Sophia embodied in Mary, who is prophetically ready to bear the Son of God in her womb. As a reward, she is wearing the halo of the Resurrected. The whole of creation is rejoicing with the choir of angels. Sophia-Mary takes an active part as a musician in the concert of the angels. Grünewald's depiction of Sophia in a blue aura has received special attention from interpreters of the work. She has been referred to as "The mother of good advice," "*Maria idealis vel aeterna*" (The ideal or eternal Mary), and the "Essence of Mary."

An interesting parallel: in *La Divina Commedia* Dante refers to the Madonna as "*la coronata fiamma*" (the crowned flame). According to G. Scheja, this representation has its origin in Byzantine times, the influence of which is also reflected in Sophia churches and icons. He holds that the baldachin reveals many things: it represents the Old Testament as "the first marriage," the *hieros gamos*, the holy wedding between God and Sophia, as it is expressed in Revelation 8:30 and Wisdom 8:3.[24]

Scheja emphasizes the influence of the Florentine Accademia Platonica on Italian Art and on the Italian Renaissance, which reaches Jacob Boehme through Paracelsus. It is indicated by the fact that Paracelsus, and Boehme also, regard Nous or Logos and the World Soul (Sophia) as the absolute ancestors. According to Scheja, it points toward the Platonic influence of "being embodied of light."[25]

The next document is the Sophia-Sapientia picture of the Church of Mary named after the Victory of Ingolstadt.[26] The church was

24. Scheja, *Isenheimer*, 41.
25. Ibid., 66.
26. Appendix X.

built as the prayer and meeting hall of the student congregation of the university between 1732 and 1737. The fresco on the back wall was painted by Cosmas Damian Asam in 1734.

The caption of the picture is a quotation: *Sapientia aedificavit sibi donum*, "Wisdom has built her house" (Prov 9:1). Accordingly, the image depicts Sapientia (Sophia) upon a throne with signs of royalty such as six lions lying before her feet. She is surrounded by the house of wisdom, which is a church. In the picture Wisdom is not represented simply as one of the seven gifts of the Holy Spirit, as in a number of other pictures; rather, based on the literature of wisdom, it is represented as an individual being (see caption). There is a holy dove hovering above Sapientia, over which there is a triangle with the eye of God. An angel holds a mirror to the dove, in which both the dove and the triangle with the eye of God are reflected. The dove in the mirror radiates light at Sophia, who is sitting on the throne.

The fresco was made in Baroque style, but in its content it is the continuation of the ancient and medieval representation of Sophia. The picture, based on Wisdom 7:12–22, represents Sophia as a queen, the artistic creator (*technitis*), the mother of the universe (*Genetis*), and the Soul of the World. We must emphasize that the picture is not about the Logos or Jesus Christ: it is about Sapientia as an individual being. This is further stressed by Sophia symbols such as the palm, the cypress, the serpent, and the mirror.[27]

The fresco makes it clear that Sophia has a special relationship with the Holy Trinity as represented by the triangle and with the Holy Spirit. The dove is the mirror or icon of the Holy Spirit, and Sophia-Mary is the reflection of God, as was later emphasized by Jakob Boehme.

In the Litany of Loreto, Mary has the following names: Ark of the Covenant, Golden House, Ivory Tower, The Gate of Heaven, Healer of the Sick,[28] and the Helper of Christ. According to some interpretations, the picture unites the figure of the Queen of Sheba, a symbol of the wisdom books, with the Greek Goddess Pallas Athena.

---

27. Schipflinger, *Sophia*, 112.

28. Similarities with the expressions used in the Marian devotion of the East, or paraklis, are surprising.

They are the prefigurations of Mary, who is the embodiment of Sophia-Sapientia.[29]

The teaching panel of the Church of Loreto in Birkenstein[30] is a continuation of the fresco in Ingolstadt. The panel painting was made by Josef Xaver Gross in 1761, thirty years after the Sapientia fresco was painted in Ingolstadt. The painting does not name Sapientia or Sophia, primarily because people would not have understood these names. Instead, it depicts Mary. However, it places one under the other as the two dimensions of Mary's being: the *"aeonian"* or heavenly Mary, in other words Sophia, and her life on earth. Therefore, it must be a representation of Sophia-Mary.

In the middle section of the panel we can see the Heavenly Sophia surrounded by angels. The source of this scene is Proverbs 8:30: "When he fixed the foundations of earth, then was I beside him as artisan; I was his delight day by day, playing before him all the while." The other source is Augustine's concept of *Sapientia creata*. The next image shows Mary and her child below Sophia. She is Sophia on earth. The painting also depicts the *epiteton ornanses* of the Litany of Loreto, similar to the grail in Ingolstadt.[31] Traditions of the representation of Sophia in the Middle Ages and through the Renaissance constitute an important part of the collective unconscious of Europe.

29. Ibid.
30. Appendix XI.
31. Schipflinger, *Sophia*, 120.

10

Jakob Boehme, Father
of Western Sophiology

JAKOB BOEHME is the father of Western sophiology, in which he examines the Trinitarian, cosmological, and mariological dimensions of Sophia. A Lutheran, he was born in Altseidenberg in 1575 and died in Görlitz in 1624 where he made his living as a simple shoemaker. While an apprentice he travelled all over Europe and became acquainted with Gnosticism. He had mystical experiences, including one in which he saw a supernatural light for seven days and was overcome by peace. He wrote his first work *Aurora* in 1610.[1] He is also regarded as the founder of Christian Theosophy (see his work *Sechs theosophische Punkte*).[2]

Boehme was greatly influenced by the physician Balthasar Walther, director of the chemical laboratory of Dresden, who had been to the Middle East in search of wisdom. Walther knew Paracelsus and was familiar with contemporary alchemy, astrology, and the Kabbalah. Through Walther, then, Paracelsus passed his knowledge on to Boehme, who said that the Greek word "idea" appeared to him in the form of a beautiful, pure, heavenly girl. It was also Walther who acquainted Boehme with Platonic teachings. Only then did Boehme become committed to Sophia, which is not yet

---

1. The following six works are of importance for our inquiry: *De tribus principiis* (*Drei Prinzipien*, The Three Principles), *De triplici vita* (The Three Types of Life), *Der Weg zu Christo* (*Die Christosophia*: The Road that Leads to Christ, or Christosophia), *Von der wahren Busse* (About Real Penitence), *De incarnatione Verbi* (About the Incarnation of the Word), and: *De signatura rerum* (The Symbolic Nature of Things).

2. Jakob Boehme, *Sämtliche Schriften*, vols. 1–11. (Stuttgart: Peukert, 1970), vol. 10: *Vita*. Not to be confused with the Theosophy of H. P. Blavatsky.

apparent in his first work. His last works are a proof of the intimate relationship he experienced with Sophia and reveal a dialogue between his soul and Sophia.

The Lutheran Church and the court of the Prince of Dresden, however, did not show much understanding toward Boehme, and he was even imprisoned for a time because of his beliefs. He was ahead of his age. His works, however, were soon translated into Russian and eventually reached Vladimir Solovyov, Nikolai Berdyaev, and Sergei Bulgakov. For a long time Boehme had little influence on the German people, but the leading figures of German idealism such as Fichte, Schelling, and Hegel drew heavily on his works. Hegel based the idea of dialectics on the *Three Principles*. He thought that Boehme's language and style were barbaric, but he borrowed a number of philosophical terms from him such as *Ungrund*, *Urgund*, and *Wesenheit*. Franz von Baader and Christoph Oetinger also borrowed much from him.

The Teaching of Boehme

The view according to which Sophia should be regarded as a person is often rejected on ecumenical grounds. However, it has been recognized in Protestant circles as well that diminishing the importance of Mary leads to a one-sided, male domination. As a result, many Protestants have become feminists. Nevertheless, many of the Protestant mystics have linked Sophia with Mary. Jakob Boehme was the first of those mystics. This is the main reason why his work is so important.

Boehme does not follow the Aristotelian-Scholastic path. He is a follower of Platonist ideas, but he also takes into consideration the teaching of Gnosticism and the Kabbalah,[3] and his work even has resonances with Taoism.[4] Boehme is almost like an existentialist searching for the meaning of life. He raises questions later taken up

---

3. Gerschom Scholem, *Von der mystischen Gestalt der Gottheit: Studien zu den Grundbegriffen der Kabbala* (Frankfurt: Conze, 1977), 135.

4. Jakob Hamberger, *Die Lehre des Deutschen Philosophen Jakob Böhme*, new edition (Hildesheim: Herder, 1975), 15.

by Heidegger: Why does the world exist and what would happen if there was nothing? What is the meaning of life?

Boehme was looking for the Ground of Being. The absolute, the ground, however, is inexpressible. Therefore, he calls it *Ungrund*, meaning "without basis" (*aseitas Dei*); something which does not need a further cause or explanation. For Boehme, it is the latent Primary Will, whose self-knowledge and freedom is absolute. As in a mirror, He sees the possible solutions and on the basis of that He decides what sort of specific reality to create.

This inward *ad intra* reflection of the basis of being (God) is the eternal divine "*Scientz*," who is "the mother of the word of all that exists." Boehme also calls it *Vorliebe*, or love before all other love, and *Wesenheit* meaning Wisdom. The outward (*ad extra*) reflection of the basis of being he calls the created image of the eternal divine mirror. This is Sophia, the idea of ideas, the entelechy of entelechies, the *arche*, the original and basic principle of creation.

Scientz is the equivalent of the Latin *scientia*, which derives from the word *scire* = "to knows, understand." It means understanding as the basis of being. It is the equivalent of the concept of Sophia = Sapientia. Boehme identifies the divine mirror, the *ad intra* reflection of the basis of being with the Holy Spirit, whose *ad extra* reflection is Sophia. She is "the mother of all that exists," which she creates together with the Holy Spirit;[5] she is "*Scientz*—the Mother, inside whom the Father acts."[6]

The self-realization and self-genesis of God take place at the most sacred depths of His being and at the most sacred depth of creation. There are qualities and latent possibilities in the *Ungrund*, which Boehme, with incorrect grammar but correctly as regards content, describes with the word *Quelle*, or Spring. It suggests qualities, polarities, the duality of good and evil.

In the light of Gnostic influences, Boehme tried to resolve the problem of evil by stating that both original principles, good and evil, are rooted in God. However, evil is not a sin but a will. God,

---

5. "Schutzschriften wider Tilken, Stiefel und Richter," II/62 in *Jakob Böhme und das Wesen seiner Mystik* (Berlin: Weissensee Verlag, 1999), 150.

6. Ibid., II/64.

who is originally pure will without an object, goes through a process of inner development, reaches self-consciousness, and wishes to create his own image. Thus consciousness (good) and will (evil) are separated from each other. As a result original sin and the world are created, which absorb all images and hold God in bondage.[7]

Boehme does not adopt Manichaeism or anything like the absolute dualism of the Indian Sankhya philosophy, whose frameworks include the "Good God" beside the "Bad God." Instead, he says that there is absolute freedom in God, which appears at the level of creatures (angels and people) in the form of hatred, sin, and evil. Freedom is part of being the image of God, but it also has unfortunate consequences. Basically, we are discussing the dialectics of evil here.

According to Boehme, suffering, mistakes, and sin have a meaning. They are signs. In the same way a toothache indicates that the tooth is decayed, mistakes indicate that our direction is wrong and we should not follow the path we have chosen. But—*errando discimus*—we can learn from our mistakes and we can emerge stronger than if we had not made these mistakes. Sin is, in the words of St. Augustine, a *felix culpa*, or joyful fault, which triggers the mercy of God and makes us even more victorious.

The Sources of the Sophia-Teaching of Boehme

Boehme's Sophia teaching had two sources: his own mystical experiences and his knowledge of history. One might think that Platonic influences had a decisive role in his way of thinking. Indeed, he does write about the idea of ideas: "especially lovely, heavenly, pure Maiden and goddess of the spirit," as Frankenberg mentions in his biography of Boehme.[8] However, Boehme always relies on his own experiences. In *Drei Prinzipien* he reports that Sophia herself appeared to him.[9]

---

7. Pál Kecskés, *A bölcselet története* [*The History of Philosophy*] (Budapest: Szent István Társulat, 1981), 257.

8. *Vita,* I/20.

9. *De tribus principiis,* II/14/52.

Jakob Boehme, Father of Western Sophiology

It is of course the historical sources that we can grasp. Boehme marks two gates: one of them is the Bible. He was familiar with scripture in the translation of Luther, who did not regard the books of Sirach and Wisdom as divinely revealed (although he acknowledged that "they are useful and good readings"). Boehme was familiar with the literature of wisdom. He quotes from it not so much word by word but according to its meaning. His favorite chapters are Proverbs 8 and Sirach 24, but he also likes to quote from Wisdom 7–9. Chapter 8 of Proverbs is particularly important to him because it describes the role of Sophia in creation.

In Sirach 24:3–6 Boehme found further proof for the theory according to which Sophia is the entelechy of entelechies not only in creation but in the sustenance of the world as well. In chapters 7 and 8 of Wisdom we find some of the most unique sources for the teaching of polarity. We can find seven characteristics of Sophia in these chapters: she is strong, mild, firm, serious, luminous, pure, and articulate. These qualities are identical with the seven qualities attributed to her by Boehme. Especially apt are the expressions that are recurrent in the Sophia teaching of Boehme: Sophia is the breath of divine strength, the mirror of God, and the image of the goodness and essence of God. Sophia is both immanent and transcendent at once, and she is present in everything that exists.

In Boehme's interpretation (based on Wisdom 7–8) Sophia's embodiment is a woman. We can call her a mother and bride. Scripture describes her beauty in great detail. She inhabits mainly the soul of the pious. She is a friend, lover, bride, master, and teacher of those who seek her. She gives the gift of immortality to those who remain faithful to her. She is the source of delight and pure desire. She is the ambassador of God and the helper and comforter of man.[10]

There are conflicting views concerning whether Sophia is only a metaphor, an allegory, a word with a mythological meaning, a virtue, a feature of God, a personification, or a real divine person. To Boehme, Sophia is definitely a person: the "noble, clean, and divine Virgin Sophia." She was born before all time and before every being. She is a *Werkmeister* who is God's partner in creation. The creator

---

10. *Christosophia*, I/45–53.

lives inside her. She is a unique being, an individual power, a person, and the Thou of God. She is an intermediary between the Creator and creation, the conductor of the orchestra of creation before the scene of God. Boehme describes her role with the same words as the Jewish Hokmah tradition describes the role of the Hokmah.[11]

We should not hide the fact that, similarly to the teaching of the Fathers (especially St. Athanasius), Boehme sometimes also refers to Sophia as a bridegroom. This is partly the continuation of the idea of meekness, but it should also be partly interpreted in accordance with the Jungian theory of bisexuality.[12] However, when Boehme expresses his own ideas, he always refers to Sophia as a woman.

Boehme's other "gate" is the sophianic tradition of the Middle Ages, which was probably influenced by the Eastern Church (see the Sophia icons), but he was also familiar with the representation of the seven *artes liberales* or seven gifts of the Holy Spirit and the visions of Hildegard of Bingen. He also knew the work of the Dominican father Heinrich Suso (1295–1366), another representative of sophianic mysticism who had mystical experiences for 18 years, after which he became the servant of Eternal Wisdom similar to the way a knight becomes the servant of a lady. He saw Sophia as a queen in a golden gown next to the throne of God and regarded himself as the lover of the queen. He held: "*Ipsa Sponsa et ego eius servulus*," "She is the bride and I am her servant." He saw the meaning of the ideal of the medieval knight in such service.

Boehme had borrowed some concepts (Malkuth, Shekinah) from the sophiology of the Kabbalah as well. He himself acknowledged that in the formulation of the concept of the *Ungrund*, the origin of evil and the theory of qualities, he was influenced by the Kabbalah. Some hold that he quotes mainly from the Kabbalah, which is not the case, as he only quotes sparingly from it.[13] But let us have a look at the sophiology of Boehme in more detail.

11. Lee Mack, *Logos*, 140.

12. Carl Gustav Jung, *Der Mensch und seine Symbole*, ed. Marie-Louise von Franz (Freiburg: Olten, 1968) and Jung, *Animus und Anima* (Zürich: Peter, 1974).

13. *La Mediatrice Cosmique: La Vierge Sophie de Jakob Böhme: L'Univers a' la Renaissance, Microcosme et Macrocosme* (Bruxelles: Presses Universitaires de Bruxelles, 1970), 145.

Jakob Boehme, Father of Western Sophiology

Boehme's "Own" Sophiology

Boehme sought the origin of Sophia in the *Ungrund*, the deepest basis of being. The *Ungrund* (the One without Basis, the Formless, Chaos) means both primary being and total being in itself. In other words, it is Being. This *Ungrund* is a mere potentiality. While realizing itself, the *Ungrund* unfolds into a *Grund*, or Basis. This basis is the absolute divine *Ens a se*, the one who originates from his own self. It is divine nature. It is represented in the form of Will and Knowledge (*Scientz*, Wisdom) and as their fruit at the same time. We can see the nature of the divine in itself, oriented toward itself (*ad intra*, inwardly). This is the life of God in the Holy Trinity. It is those certain "three original principles" in the sphere of divine existence.[14]

However, this divine Trinity wants to express itself outwards (*ad extra*) as well. This is what takes place in creation. According to Boehme, the ancestral image of creation is Created Wisdom, Sophia, the unique image of uncreated divine Wisdom, and she is the Mother Spirit. She is the one who contains and carries the essence of all created things. God learns about them as possible forms of being in the mirror of the created Sophia.

Therefore, Sophia is the beginning, the original principle of creation (*Resit = Arche*) with the help of whom (*bo-resit*) God created heaven and earth and the entire universe (Gen 1:1). Therefore, Sophia is the Co-creator, the mother of the world and the cosmos, and a divine mediator between God and the world. She is the partner and helper of the Son in His redeeming and saving work. She also helps the Son become man. Her contribution consists in assuming a human form as she becomes flesh and blood in Mary and in her motherhood she serves the incarnation of the Son with her own flesh and blood.

The Components of Boehme's Sophiology

1. Eternal Divine Wisdom in the Holy Trinity

Boehme always thinks in terms of a trinity, which is revealed by the title of his two major works: *De tribus principiis* and *De triplici vita*.

---

14. Aimé Koyré, *La philosophie de Jakob Böhme* (Paris: Cerf, 1971), 78.

He holds that the starting point is the Monas, the Hen; unity that becomes duality and polarity and eventually the duality becomes Oneness again. According to Boehme, the first Triassic is the divine Trinity, whose starting point is the divine Original Basis, the divine essence that becomes polarity (Will = Father and *Scientz*-Wisdom = Holy Trinity, Mother Spirit) and whose fruit is the Son.

This interpretation is different from the interpretation of classical dogmatics, according to which the Holy Spirit (in Western interpretation) originates from the Father and the Son, or (in the Eastern interpretation) from the Father alone. Boehme accepted the traditional interpretation, but his triadist-polarist approach goes beyond its boundaries. He describes the internal process of the Holy Trinity as follows:

> God did not have an image in whom He could have seen His own self. It has become possible only now, through Wisdom. She has become His delight. [...] Therefore this virgin, Wisdom, is the image of God in whom the spirit of God can see himself.[15]
>
> It is Nothingness that makes the Will want to have an image, and as a result the Will can see Himself in the mirror of Wisdom. [...] And the Image is conceived by Wisdom, a virgin mirror, because she (the mirror) is a mother.[16]

By "Nothingness," Boehme means that God has nothing and nobody to make him happy. It means the Not Yet Existing, the Partner, the Son, whom He deeply desires. The emphasis on desire is unusual, especially in a theological setting. In Hinduism, by contrast, every desire is the source of suffering. Desire is far away from the world of the spirit and therefore men should avoid it. Here, however, it is the key concept of divine being. But we know that Yahweh is a jealous god and *eros* is not far from the Judeo-Christian concept of God. The Father in the Gospel also talks about His beloved and loving Son (Matt 3:17).

To put it more simply, the Son is the image of the Will of the Father, the Sophia (Holy Spirit), the mirror. The Father begets and

---

15. *De incarnatione Verbi*, I/1/12.
16. Ibid., II/2/1.

reflects the Son with the help of Sophia: "Will, meaning the Father, reveals His strength [= Himself] through the mirror of Wisdom and launches the Word of life in the mirror of Wisdom."[17]

And here we should not think about the influence of Gnosticism alone. The theme of reflection is present even in the most Orthodox theology. In the Creed of Nicaean-Constantinopolitan, the image of physical reflection is used to describe the relationship between the Father and the Son (Light of Light). Jesus Christ himself says: "Those who see me see the Father" (John 14:9). Biological reflection is also present in the Creed and in the best known trinitologies (in the concept of the Father and the Son). A number of theologians extend the process of reflection to the three divine persons. The Cappadocian Fathers say that the Father is like the Sun, and the Son is like the light. The Holy Spirit is the moon that makes this "reflection of light" possible.

But let us return to Boehme. *Scientz* is a key concept in the teaching of Boehme. This concept includes not only the Latin word *scientia*, or science, but it also includes the meaning of the words *cieo* = starts, move, pull, cause, and create. He expresses this meaning with the German word *ziehen* (pull, draw, establish). This etymology helps us to understand the causal role of *Scientz*.

For Boehme, "*Scientz* is the original cause because of which the divine will (the Father) constricts (encompasses) itself and expresses itself in nature (the Heart, the Word, and the Son)."[18] The Kabbalah also mentions that for Yahweh creation is a form of self-restraint or self-pruning (*kenosis* in the terminology of the New Testament). It seems that Boehme was familiar with that idea.

Scientz, the phenomenon of Sophia, has two directions: *ad intra* and *ad extra*. *Ad intra*: "Eternal *Scientz* forces the will (whom we call the Father) to concentrate in the center of the divine birth of the Trinity and pronounce the Word of Intelligence (= the Logos) with *Scientz*."[19] Boehme adds that, "The other *Scientz* is the root of every spiritual beginning. It is the true root of the soul and every life

17. Ibid., II. 62/2–3.
18. *Schlüssel zu den wichtigsten Wörtern*, 144.
19. Ibid., 145.

because it is of the Basic Source of Life from which it originates."[20] Boehme holds that this second *Scientz* is the image of the eternal divine *Scientz*, or created wisdom: Sophia.

Some hold that Boehme believed not in the Trinity but in *Vierfältigkeit* or Fourness. He believed that *Scientz* was a fourth principle beside the three divine persons. However, Boehme places *Scientz*-Sophia not next to the three divine persons as a fourth one but identifies it with the Holy Spirit. Even if his approach is different from that of traditional trinitology, he believes in the Trinity. What is unique is that he provides not only dogmas but a theory of being as well, which is the ontogenetic principle of the Trinity: Unity-duality-trinity. Even if he strays from the traditional path or resorts to Gnosticism, he has a uniquely important role in the discovery of the maternal face of God.

2. *Divine Wisdom (Sophia) in Creation*

In Boehme's view, Wisdom is not only the key element of reflection within the Holy Trinity, but God Himself (and thus the entire Trinity as well) is reflected by it in the whole of creation. He recognizes the possible forms of being through Sophia and it is her (the Holy Spirit, the Mother Spirit) *fiat* or affirmation that gives birth to what exists. As it is expressed in Proverbs 8:22: "The Lord possessed me (the created Sophia) in the beginning of his way (= as the *arche* of things), before his works of old."

Here Sophia is at the center of cosmogonic relationships: "It is the same Virgin, Wisdom, who is at the center of the secret [the secret of creation]. The spirit of God saw in her the forming principle of His creatures. The Logos, the Spoken Word [Word = the creating Word][21] which is pronounced by the Father from the Word of the Divinity [= Logos] together with the Holy Spirit, originates from her. She is like a window or mirror before the scene of the Lord."[22] He also compares Sophia the Co-Creator to clothing. He calls her

20. Ibid., 143.
21. "Everything was created by him (the Logos) and nothing was created without him" (John 1:3).
22. *De incarnatione*, I. 61/12.

the *Sichtbarkeit* (visible reality) and *Leiblichkeit* (the bodily side) of the heavenly Sophia.[23]

And here we can find an interesting parallel to scripture. In Paul's letter to the Ephesians Christ is the center of creation ("According as he had chosen us before the foundation of the world, that we should be holy and without blame before him in love" [Eph 1:4]). Boehme, however, chooses Sophia as the foundation of creation (understood as a reflection): "Divine Wisdom became visible in this eternal mirror, which was given to the creature in the beginning in the Fiat said to God."[24] Not only the fate of man was formed in the mirror of Sophia, but the fate of the world as well: "The essence of this world (as a third principle) became visible in this Mirror."[25]

Boehme sees the cosmologic-cosmonomic Sophia as a mother: "Sophia is the mother of all that exists. She is the Matrix who, as a single image, contains the skies, the stars, the elements, the earth, and all that moves and is alive."[26] "The essence of what exists becomes visible in her. She is the great miracle, the eternal original element in whom every essence becomes visible thousands of times and forever. She is the mother in whom the Father works. She is the mother of all that exists, to which she gives birth together with the Holy Spirit (= Mother Spirit) and which she creates with the Fiat of the Word (= the Son)."[27] Elsewhere he says: "She is the mother of all that exists, the force which forms the holy ground."[28] "She is the one who provides life and leads the world."[29]

Sophia is the life-giver and the leader of the world. But how is it possible? Boehme often compares the work of Sophia to the "work of the soul in the body." People have three levels of soul: the spiritual soul (*anima spiritualis*), the sensory soul (*anima sensitiva*), and the bodily soul, which lead, sustain, and control the body, as biologists

---

23. *De triplici vita*, 3, 49.
24. *Schutzschriften*, I/148.
25. Ibid., I/142.
26. *De triplici vita*, 11/13.
27. *Schutzschriften wider Tilken, Stiefel und Richter*, II/64–65.
28. *De tribus principiis*, 22/41.
29. Ibid., 5/49–53.

would say. In the same way, Sophia also moves the universe at three levels. The spiritual soul of the world Boehme calls *Geist Majoris Mundi*, the Soul of the macrocosm. This is what governs the skies, the deepest foundations. The feeling soul he calls *archaeus* (in the same way as the word *Archaea* is used in Russian sophiology), from which the four elements arise: the sky visible to us (sun, moon, stars, and the planets) is born. The bodily soul of the world Boehme calls *Spiritus Mundi*, or World Spirit, which constitutes the basis of the individual elements. Today it would be referred to as the Soul of the Ecological System.

Boehme's sophianic cosmology can be summarized by saying the (created) Sophia is a creature of God, the mirror in which God sees His creative ideas and *ad extra* possibilities. Sophia is the Idea of Ideas, which contains the idea of all creatures. She realizes God's ideas according to His decisions (Wisdom 8:4), provides them with a visible material form, gives birth to them, and sustains them. She is the Mother of Creation. These material realities are her body and she is their soul. She is the soul of the universe; she is the World Soul. We can learn about her strength and beauty from the world and in the world, and through her we can learn about the strength and beauty of the Creator.

According to this grand vision, creation and the cosmos are the body and clothing of Sophia (as we have seen it with the concept of Nothing). Sophia is the soul of the world; nature is her body, expression, and secret code. This is what constitutes the basis of Boehme's nature mysticism. Unlike modern day exploitative attitudes lacking any humility toward nature, Boehme's treatment of nature inspires respect for the Mother of the World and the Earth. Honor your (Father and) Mother.[30]

3. *Sophia's Relationship with Mary*

The relationship of Sophia and Mary constitutes the most interesting and most original part of Boehme's sophiology. It holds that

---

30. Schipflinger, *Sophia*, 132.

Sophia became human in the body of Mary. She is the bridgehead in a cold and disintegrating world on which a new Eden can be built. She is the divine womb that gave birth to the Son, the Incarnation of God.

The sophiology-mariology of Boehme asserts that "Sophia was chosen to become one with Mary, to give her strength and to prepare her for becoming the mother of the Logos that became man. She incarnated herself in Mary, and Mary is the incarnate Sophia."[31] "Mary is the beautiful earthly virgin who becomes one with the divine Virgin, Sophia."[32] "Sophia, whom the Father had planted into Mary, became human in Mary."[33] Boehme is also familiar with the *hieros gamos* of the Logos and Sophia: "Sophia married the Son, the heart of God, in the presence of the Father."[34]

Boehme had hardly any historical sources.[35] His main source must have been Valentin Weigel, whom he sometimes refers to, or the literature of wisdom (although as a Protestant he must have known that Luther declared several of these apocryphal). He might have found some references in the Book of Baruch as well: "Thus she [Wisdom] has appeared on earth, and is at home among men" (Baruch 3:38). The Kabbalah cannot have referred to Mary. Unfortunately his teaching has been neglected by Catholic theology so far. However, it can be very relevant today in the age of ecumenism, for it can refute those views according to which mariology should be marginalized according to Protestantism.

The Sophiology and Importance of Boehme

Boehme must have resorted mainly to his own visions. His work *Christosophia* is a strong indication of that. Here he says that Sophia represents the same thing to him as to Solomon: a teacher, bride,

---

31. *De incarnatione Verbi*, I/8, 2.
32. Ibid., I/8, 12.
33. *De tribus principiis*, 22/38.
34. Ibid., 18/41.
35. Schipflinger, *Sophia*, 133.

and guide (Wisdom 8:2–18). In this work he describes the dialogue between Sophia and his own soul (= every pure soul) several times.

As Boehme writes in *Christosophia*, "The noble Sophia says encouragingly to the spirit: ah my noble groom. Be sure that I am committed to you in my love and bound to you in faithfulness. I wish to be by your side and inside you to the end of the world and I want to inhabit your innermost being. You must drink from my spring; then I will be yours and you will be mine."[36] This is the world of the most intimate Sophia mysticism. Boehme's sources must have been Hosea 11:4 and Ephesians 5:32 where scripture describes the relationship between Yahweh and the people of Israel, a description also apparent in the Song of Songs.

In traditional Christian mysticism the bridegroom is Christ and his bride is Mary, the Church collectively, and the individual souls. This spiritual unity has a fundamental role in the ideal of monastic life. Boehme, however, refers to the opposite of that. He holds that the bride is Sophia and her embodiment is Mary and the Church. This role of Sophia is the role envisioned by Solomon. It is the role of the mother, the *anagoga* (the female leader), akin to Beatrice who fosters the fulfilment of the male spirit (or animus according to Jung).

Based on the above, Boehme should be regarded as the father of Western sophiology. His work is an ecumenical phenomenon which can serve as a source of inspiration and encouragement for the following:

1. Eastern sophiology to accept its own sophiology more confidently.

2. The Catholic Church to integrate the sophiology of the Bible into its own mariology and pneumatology.

3. The Churches of the Reformation to find a way to the discovery of the feminine dimension of God through Mary.

4. Anyone seeking wisdom (philo-sophia) and who might find encouragement in the words of Sophia in *Christosophia*: "I will be

---

36. *Christosophia*, 51.

inside you and by your side to the end of the world. […] We would like to stay in your church, which is ourselves. Amen."[37]

Finally, what does Boehme have to say to us today? His work is a milestone, though often complicated by the strikingly original revelations and confusing images from a simple shoemaker who became one of the great thinkers of his age and yet had little influence on it. But what is his message? It comes down to two things: (1) *that Being (Sein) has a polar structure and it includes both good and evil*; and (2) *that Sophia, as a principle of life, is present at every level of existence.*

Let us have a look at all that in more detail. Every form of being, even divine being (*Sein*), originates from the *Ungrund*,[38] which is a dynamic, creative, and entirely free original basis. This dynamic basic principle gave birth to polarities such as darkness and light, water and fire, and hardness and softness. Reality was born out of the mixture of these. Evil is not so much a quality in itself. Rather, it is an unbalanced mixture of polar qualities and the components of being.

The existence of such an inferior mixture is due to the freedom of those who exist and are endowed with a spirit as well as to the limited and finite nature of things. The first maculate mixture is represented by Lucifer, who used his freedom improperly and rebelled against God. As a result, other creatures were born who intentionally went the wrong way and triggered the entire drama of Evil.

The idea of the ontological polarity of being became alienated from Western thought. As a result, the idea of Wisdom as a comprehensive view directed at the whole was replaced by a one-sided, monolithic, static, and individualistic way of thinking. And here a mistaken approach surfaces again: contrasting the rational with the intuitive, the individual with the collective, material with the spirit, freedom with structure, the unique with holistic. This is the primary reason for the one-sided development of Western societies,

---

37. Ibid., 52.

38. Which may be equivalent to the concept of divine *Dynamis* in Eastern theology.

which could lead to ecological disaster and the nuclear destruction of the world. Boehme repeats it over and over again: polarities and polar opposites constitute an integral part of the dynamic existence of being.

Boehme holds that everything that exists has an invisible inner life, a soul. The soul is the life and forming principle of all things. It determines the external form of things, or "signature" as Boehme calls it. He talks about it in detail in *Signatura rerum*. The external forms of visible things are the external signs of internal realities. They are comprehensible reflections of internal determiners. They are the incarnations of a principle. This was and probably still is referred to with the words *entelechia* and *physis*, *noumenon* and *phainomenon*, or spirit and appearance.

Sophia is the highest *entelechia*, the highest artist. The world is her body, clothing, and signature. She is the password that opens all doors and reveals the secrets of nature. She is the Soul and Spirit of the World. She is the representation of the internal and external life of both plants and animals. She is everything that has a spirit. That is, she has a spiritual relationship with nature and inspires an awe of nature. This provides a spiritual basis for such principles as the protection of the environment and the fight against the exploitation and depletion of our natural resources.

Concerning polarities, Sophia is the one who directs our relationship with the Creator into the right channels. She always uses her freedom and power to promote the interests of the Whole as well as the interests of the individual. She harmonizes polarities. She is the Woman of Peace. She is an Artist aiming at beauty and perfection. According to both Eastern and Western tradition, Sophia-Mary is the Queen of Paradise. She teaches people wisdom and the fulfilment of love. And we know that that is what Heaven is.

Freedom should not be interpreted as something stagnant and inflexible. Rather, freedom should be considered as something dynamic; it means being able to adapt to new situations. It is something holistic, universal, and integral. The correct application of freedom means adjusting to the designs of God and Sophia. The strength to do so may be gained from prayer and cooperation.

Boehme often compares Sophia to a mirror in which God can see

Himself, and in which He is pleased by what He sees. The mirror reflects the light at an angle from which it is not visible directly. God is invisible (John 1:18), but now He becomes visible through His Son and the partner of the Logos, Sophia. We can also become mirrors with the help of Sophia to become "the visible icons of God the invisible" together with Christ.[39]

39. Schipflinger, *Sophia*, 137.

11

Western Prophets of Sophia in the Modern Age

The Philadelphian Society

JAKOB BOEHME had a great influence on English religious life between 1650 and 1750. Charles I (reigned 1625–1649) was himself interested in Boehme's teaching. Most of Boehme's works were translated into English within twenty-five years of his death. He had a particularly strong influence on John Pordage, a vicar in London at the end of the seventeenth century. Pordage's main works are *Theologia mystica*, *Metaphysica divina*, *Sophia*, and *Philosophia mystica*. He was a follower of Boehme in cosmology and in the theory of redemption, but he had his own ideas concerning salvation. He held that our goal was resurrection, but first we should be united to and cooperate with Sophia. "Christ must be born, live, suffer, die and resurrect inside of us by Sophia."[1]

Another English disciple of Boehme was Jane Lead (1623–1670).[2] In her diary she reports that "Sophia appeared to me in the form of a very friendly and graceful woman, in lightning, similarly to how the Sun radiates in her transparent golden clothing." Sophia appeared to Lead in different forms: in the form of a queen with a crown of stars surrounded by angels; as the woman dressed in sun-

---

1. "J. Pordage," in *Realencyklopädie für protestantische Theologie und Kirche* Bd. 15 (Leipzig: Chores, 1913), 553.

2. Her works include *The Heavenly Cloud Now Breaking* (1681), *The Revelation of Revelations* (1683), *A Fountain of Gardens* (1701), *The Laws of Paradise* (1695), *A Message to the Philadelphia Society* (1696), *A Revelation of the Everlasting Gospel Message* (1697), and *The Ascent to the Mount of Vision* (1698).

light from Revelation; as one of the characteristics or powers of God whose secrets are hidden by a book; and as a divine principle in whose soul one must be born similarly to the way Christ must be born inside us, in accord with the saying of Angelus Silesius: "Even if Christ is born a thousand times in Bethlehem, but not inside of you, you will remain lost forever."[3] In 1670 Lead founded the *Philadelphian Society* with Pordage, which did a great deal to make Sophia better known.

Lead teaches that Sophia is the guardian and mediator of the secrets of God. She is a divine principle, an idea, a form, and a pattern that helps people to fully realize themselves, and she has a cosmological as well as an anthropological role. Sophia creates divine harmony in people; therefore, she is a mother and a helper. A "Sophianic Rebirth" takes place through her and, as a result, a unique "Sophianic community" is born. The goal is the "divination of the earth" and the creation of the ultimate man, the perfect man who is androgynous, that is, who unites the internal characteristics of both sexes (an idea in harmony with the Jungian idea of animus-anima).

According to his commentators (Ernst Benz, Solovyov), Boehme signals the time of the arrival of the Holy Spirit: "A new spiritual land has arrived; it is before the doors." In this land those who are reborn will form a community, the community of brotherly love, a Philadelphian community where they will be living together with Christ and Sophia.[4]

The Views of Gottfried Arnold Concerning Divine Wisdom

Gottfried Arnold (1714–1707) was a Protestant mystic, a historian of religion, and a superintendent in Perleberg.[5] He called himself an evangelical sophiologist. He was one of the most gifted, intelligent, and efficient disciples of Boehme. He devoted 156 poems to Sophia and he wrote prayers to her as well.

---

3. Angelus Silesius, *Der Cherubinische Wandersmann*, I/61.
4. Edward Benz, *Vision* (Stuttgart: Master, 1969), 571.
5. His works: *Unpartheyische Kirchen- und Kertzerhistorie, Das Geheimnis der Göttlichen Sophia.*

Western Prophets of Sophia in the Modern Age

In his book *On Divine Sophia* Arnold relies on scripture and on the "writings of teachers of late." He subtitles the work "Glorifying and loving confessions concerning eternal Wisdom inspired by the 'Song of Songs.'" He reveals that Sophia appeared to him, and he expresses his love for her inspired by the Song of Songs. He addresses her as *Sulamit* and calls her his young mistress, the source of delight, and queen. He accounts for his feelings saying, "Scripture provides a sound basis for calling Wisdom not only a mother but a virgin, bride, partner and playmate as well." He refers to Wisdom 8:1 and the Song of Songs because they speak about the love of the spirit with Sophia.

Arnold quotes from the Church Fathers, especially from the Augustine of the *Confessions*: "Sophia is a wonderful divine being who is bound by such love to God that although she is not eternal as He is, she never leaves His side due to a change in space or time and she contemplates His internal essence." For Arnold, Sophia is the Augustinian *Sapientia Creata*: "Created Wisdom, or intelligent nature, who is light herself because she herself is contemplating light [...], she is the eternal spiritual home of God which has to remain immaculate forever. She is the place where the glory of the Lord dwells. [...] She is the creature of creatures, the bride of God."[6]

Arnold holds that Sophia is a person: "The above imply that Wisdom is an independent, spiritual, lasting, divine, and heavenly being who is responsible for herself." He follows the school of thought (Palamitism) that regards Sophia as the acme of the created world: "A number of holy men believe that heavenly Wisdom is not just simply a name, but it is a divine being who is above every angelic or human spirit." As Sinaita Anastasius puts it: she has independence and individuality.[7]

Although he remains within the conceptual framework created by Augustine and regards the cosmic Sophia as a created being different from both the Logos and the Holy Spirit, Arnold puts her "in line with the Holy Spirit." "She can only be moved by the eternal

6. Gottfried Arnold, *Das Geheimnis der Göttlichen Sophia*, chap. 15. Citing *Confessions* 12 and 15.
7. Chap. 31.

119

Spirit of God, whose body [...] is the reflection of the glory of God."
He is not far from the idea according to which Sophia is a reflection
of the Holy Spirit, even if she is not identical with the Holy Spirit.

Arnold was a great sophianic master, the greatest after Boehme in
Western Christianity. Unfortunately, he was unable to break
through the conceptual boundaries of his age. He lacked the mariological and theological dimensions. He was, however, a great source
of inspiration for his fellow countrymen such as Herder and
Goethe, the Russians (Solovyov and Florensky), and he accomplished a great deal in the fields of asceticism and mysticism.

The Disciples of Boehme

Johann Georg Gichtel (1638–1710), a contemporary of Arnold, was
one of the disciples of Boehme, and it would be accurate to call him
a Theosophist. His main work, *Theosophia Practica*, was published
after his death in Leyden in 1772. Gichtel was concerned with the
relationship between the created Sophia and the Holy Spirit. In his
view, Sophia is a mirror and a womb (matrix) in whom God contemplates and realizes His designs. Sophia is the bride and man is
the bridegroom. Human persons, therefore, become part of a *hieros
gamos* through her and as a result become similar to Jesus Christ,
due to the indwelling of the Holy Spirit.

Gichtel tried to delineate practical interpretations of his experiences with Sophia, in what is called "Practical Theosophy." The
stages of this approach are comprised of understanding, entering
the realm of Sophia, and rebirth. Sophia increases the new life inside
individuals. Persons are free: if they resist, Sophia leaves them. If
they open up to her, she returns and the Trinitarian way of life is
realized. In his work, Gichtel sometimes identifies Sophia with
Christ based on the teachings of the Church Fathers and the logosophic answer of Augustine, although Schipflinger holds that he
might be referring to the anima side of Christ.[8]

Louis-Claude de Saint Martin (1743–1803) was a French philosopher, and the French translator of Boehme. First he translated the

8. Schipflinger, *Sophia*, 152.

word Sophia as *"l'homme-esprit"* (the human spirit) because this expression was very much missing from French intellectual life. He used the conceptual system of Boehme and Gichtel to hold that Sophia is the womb of becoming spiritual, an intermediary between God and the world. She is the mirror through which God contemplates the world, a form, the idea of ideas, and the ideal of humanity. Cosmologically she is the mother and soul of the world, while the world is the son and child of Sophia. All these concepts are already familiar to us.

This World-Soul is both transcendent and immanent at the same time. It is not only transcendent in the way God is transcendent in traditional Theism, nor is it only immanent in the Pantheist sense of the word. Rather, it is the unity of the two. Saint Martin also expresses a deep sense of nature mysticism. The mariological dimension appears again: in the same way as the Logos became man in Christ, Sophia was born in Mary. He also uses the idea of bride and bridegroom: Sophia is the bride of every soul.

Johann Jakob Wirz (1778–1858) was another disciple of Boehme. He was a German mystic whose works were published in two volumes under the title *Offenbarungen* in Basel in 1863.[9] He was the founder of the Nazarene Community and thought that the role model of the Nazarenes should be Mary, the incarnation of Sophia. They are like body and soul to each other. Wirz also influenced the Catholic tradition of Marian devotion through Ludwig Maria Grignon von Monforton (Louis-Marie Grignion de Montfort).[10] Indeed, St. Maximilian Kolbe and Pope Saint John Paul II both drew on the spirituality of de Montfort. It is expressed in the motto: *Totus tuus.*

Sophia in the Visions of Anne Catherine Emmerich

Although she was not a direct disciple of Boehme, Anne Catherine Emmerich (1774–1824) may be listed here as well. She was a great

---

9. Ernst Siaelin, *Der Basler Seidenweber Johann Jakob Wirz als Hellseher und Gründer der Nazarenergemeinde* (Basel: Basler Stadtbuch, 1966), 69.

10. Ludwig Maria Grignon von Monforton, *Das Goldene Buch der Vollkommenen Andacht zu Maria* (Friebourg: Kanisius, 1918).

visionary and mystic who received the stigmata in 1812. In the 18th and 19th centuries the veneration of Sophia gained dominance in the Catholic Church. It happened not so much on a sophiological basis, although we have seen examples of that, and such a view is supported by the influence of Emmerich.

It is Sophia-Mary who stands at the center of Emmerich's visions. In the records of her visions, Emmerich distinguishes between Mary the finite and Mary the infinite. She describes the birth of Mary the infinite as a process where "our breath forms a little cloud in front of our mouth. That is how her figure was born in the presence of the most Holy Trinity." Mary (the finite) is the embodiment of the infinite Virgin and the incarnation of Sophia.

In one of Emmerich's visions an angel heralds the news of the conception of Mary to St. Anne in a dream. She wrote her name on the wall in golden letters. When Joachim and Anne embraced each other, they were covered by a bright cloud. Catherine saw the preparation of the conception. She saw the Virgin through God, and in God. She also saw the creation of the soul of Mary and its unification with the most pure body of Mary. The symbols used by Emmerich such as the throne, mirror, cloud, vessel, tower, breeze, gem, mountain, and bean are all present in sophianic literature.

Thus Anne Catherine Emmerich is the third most significant sophiologist in the West next to Jakob Boehme and Gottfried Arnold. She is primarily the witness of the mariological dimension of Sophia. The first part of her visions was published in a book called *The Sufferings of Jesus Christ* in 1833. The second part was published in *The Life of the Virgin Mary* (*Das Leben der heiligen Jungfrau Maria*) in 1852, a modern edition of which was printed in 1964 and 1992 in a run of eighty-five-thousand copies.[11] In 2004 John Paul II beatified Emmerich, and now she stands with Sophia in the heavenly choir of the saints.

11. See also the recent, definitive, supplemented, edition: *The Visions of Anne Catherine Emmerich*, 3 vols., ed. James Richard Wetmore (Kettering, OH: Angelico Press, 2015).

12

Sophiology in Russian Religious Philosophy

Vladimir Solovyov, the Father of Russian Sophiology

RESEARCH carried out by Western sophiologists did not prove to be particularly successful because the Enlightenment and industrialization brought about a practical approach with all of its disadvantages. In the East, on the other hand, especially among the Russian people, the Sophia teaching had its prophets. Vladimir Solovyov was the first of such prophets; therefore, he is also called the father of Russian Sophiology.[1]

Vladimir Sergeyevich Solovyov was born in Moscow in 1853 and died in Uskoye in 1900. He was raised in accordance with the traditions of the Russian Orthodox Church, though during secondary school he became a radical atheist and materialist. Later he returned to religion and he focused mainly on sophiology. He was inspired primarily by the Sophia icons of Kiev and Novgorod and was also influenced by the piety of the Russian people, who referred to the earth as Mother Earth. As he wrote of the Sophia of Novgorod, who was so dear to him: "Who is she who has a throne and possesses the dignity of a queen if not Holy Wisdom, the real, pure humanity itself? She is the highest of all-encompassing entelechy, the living soul of nature and the universe who has merged with God for ever and who connects herself with everything that exists in time."[2]

---

1. Wladimir Solowjew, *Sophia* (Alther: Kairo, 1876).
2. Erich Klum, *Natur, Kunst und Liebe in der Philosophie Wladimir Solovjews* (München: Barth, 1965), 273.

Solovyov experienced a vision of Sophia in 1862 as a child during the Divine Liturgy. Later, he studied the literature of wisdom in the Old Testament, the Gnostic Sophia speculations, and the teachings of Boehme, Arnold, Gichtel, and Swedenborg, and he was also influenced by Oetinger, von Baader, and Schelling. Solovyov became familiar with Baron Christian Knorr von Rosenroth's *Cabbala Denudata* in London. He experienced his second vision of Sophia there in 1875, followed by a third soon thereafter in Egypt. There, at the foot of the pyramids, he became aware of the beauty of Sophia. He founded his Sophia-teaching in lectures concerning the divine nature of man and in his book *Russia and the Universal Church*. He also wrote poems in which he calls Sophia his lady and queen.

Solovyov held that the Russian people gave a new meaning to this ideal, which was unknown to the Greek Fathers who identified Sophia with the Logos. For Solovyov, Sophia connects the masculine ideal, the Logos, with the feminine ideal: sensitivity and perfect form, the representation of beauty. According to the principle of *contradictio in adiecto*, the Logos is identical with Sophia, but it is also different from her. Christ is Wisdom, but Wisdom is not the Logos. Divine Wisdom (Sophia) and the creative intellect (Logos) are embodied by Christ but they are also related to the Holy Spirit who opens up in the Divine Mother before us. The Logos and the Holy Spirit both take part in the creation of the world: "By the LORD's word the heavens were made; by the breath of his mouth all their host" (Psalm 33:6).[3]

August Comte observes that in Solovyov's work, "Nature is not simply the sum of individual beings and things; it is not an abstract idea; it is not an empirical aggregate. Rather, it is a real living being. It is a superhuman being. It is not just an embodied principle, but a principal person or personal principle. It is not just an idea, but a personal ideal [...] a Female being."[4] To Solovyov, Sophia is the universal and individual origin of every form of being and the Mother of every being. As such, she is the basis of the development of the

3. Zoltán Hajnády, *Sophia és Logosz* [*Sophia and Logos*] (Debrecen: University of Debrecen, 2002), 255.
4. Klum, *Natur*, 262.

universe and mankind. Therefore, our development may be further promoted by learning more about Sophia.

Solovyov also regards Sophia as the soul of creation, the intelligent collective soul of humanity. She has a uniting, connecting, and controlling function. He holds, probably due to the influence of Boehme, that similarly to our soul, the Sophia-World Soul also consists of three parts: the upper, heavenly part; the lower, earthly part; and the soul that is between the two functioning as a cause. This concept of Solovyov's had a great influence on the natural philosophy of the 20th century. Modern pioneers of the natural sciences have also reached a conclusion according to which the universe was created by an intelligent being similar to an organism, and many identify this concept of Sophia with the Gaia-hypothesis. Indeed, natural scientists learned sooner about it than theologians.

Solovyov connects the concept of man and Sophia with the idea of syzygy or coupled existence. While Sophia is embodied by the world, the idea is embodied by physical existence. It is all about the all-encompassing presence of polarity, the duality and nuptial structure of being where the place and meaning of the Sophia principle is apparent. According to Solovyov, pairs, polarities, and the laws of harmony constitute the driving force of the development of the world.

Divine Wisdom in Florensky's Work

Pavel Alexandrovich Florensky was born in Tiflis in 1882 and most likely he died as a martyr in St. Petersburg (at that time Leningrad) in 1937.[5] His main work is *The Pillar and Ground of the Truth*, and it is the chapter of this work entitled "Sophia" with which we are mainly interested. In this chapter Florensky writes that, as revealed in icons of Sophia, Divine Wisdom is the living soul of nature and

---

5. According to the latest research he was taken to the island of Solovky, Eastern Siberia, and from there to Leningrad in November 1937, where he was tried and executed. Today we can read the contents of the records of his trial: "The death sentence pronounced by the three member committee of the NKVD [the forerunner of the KGB] was carried out on 8 December, 1937."

the universe that unites the entire created world. Similarly to the way the persons of the Holy Trinity are consubstantial, creatures are also different but of the same substance. The unifying principle is Sophia. This highest of all beings is the Wisdom of God. Therefore, Sophia is the root of the sum of all creatures, a guardian angel, and formative basis. She is the eternal bride of the Logos. She diversifies in the ideas of creation, for which she gains her strength from the Logos. On the one hand, she is in God; on the other hand, she exists in creation. Therefore, she is the house of God, His church, and His holy city, Jerusalem. These images are familiar from the Marian poetry of the Eastern Church.

Florensky's most important direct source is Count Speransky, a Russian mystical poet from the beginning of the 19th century who worked out the Sophia-Eve analogy: similarly to the way Eve was created from the side of Adam, Sophia was created from the Logos. Just like the Holy Spirit, she is also the bride of the Logos. According to Speransky, Sophia is the daughter of the Father, the bride and sister of the Son, and the image of the Holy Spirit. She is the original principle and the mother of all that is outside of God. She is the first being after God. She is the divine Eve who is the mother of the ideas of creation.

Florensky's other source is scripture. He uses images from the Old Testament to describe the nature of Sophia: the City of God, the Heavenly Jerusalem, and the bride of Sion. He also uses images from the New Testament such as the Bride of the Lamb, that is, the Church. Like St. Clement and the Shepherd of Hermas he believes that since Sophia is the bride of God we have to accept her pre-existence; but at the same time, using the words of Augustine, he calls her *sapientia creata*.

Florensky was familiar with a number of the mariological and ecclesiastical functions of Sophia: first created, first redeemed, and the heart of redeemed creation. She is the Church. She is the sum of those who constitute the body of Christ. Furthermore, Sophia is virginity itself. In other words, she is the force by which someone can become holy. Mary is the person who is the embodiment of all these qualities; therefore, she is the incarnation of Sophia.

He concludes that Sophia = the whole of creation = humanity =

the soul and consciousness of the world. If humanity = Church, then Sophia is the soul and consciousness of humanity. If Church = church of the saints, then she is the Church of Heaven, the soul and consciousness of the Church. Since she is the soul of the Church of Heaven, she is the prime mediator of the Logos, the Judge, since she is the mother of God. Consequently she is identical with Mary.[6]

Here we should refer back to what we have said concerning the Greek liturgy. Florensky applies the attributes of the Akathist Hymn to Mary-Sophia: the bearer of joy, the leader of the world, queen of heaven and earth, the most beautiful flower of the earth, a wall that cannot be demolished, heaven of mercy, and bearer of Wisdom. She is a bridge between God and creation; she is the center and summit of creation. She is the embodiment of the Church. It has been proved again: *lex orandi, lex credendi*.

The Sophiology of Bulgakov

Sergei Nikolayevich Bulgakov was born in Livny in 1871 and died in Paris in 1944. He was an Orthodox priest and a professor at the Saint Sergius Institute in Paris. His dogmatic trilogy about the divine nature of man consists of *The Lamb of God* (Christology), *The Comforter* (Pneumatology), and *The Bride of the Lamb* (Dogmatics). His Mariology is expressed in *The Burning Bush* and *The Sophia of God*.[7]

According to Bulgakov, Sophia did not receive enough attention from theologians primarily due to logosophic interpretation, even though the Russián churches point toward a mariological dimension. The Church of Kiev, for example, was consecrated in remembrance of the birth of Mary and the Church of Novgorod was consecrated in remembrance of her Assumption. Bulgakov was influenced by the school of Boehme. He also respected Solovyov, but he believed that Solovyov had Gnostic tendencies. Basically, he regarded the principle of Sophia as a Russian idea.

Bulgakov's starting point is his conviction that man is aided by

6. Schipflinger, *Sophia*, 228.
7. *La sagesse de Dieu* (Lausanne: Icon, 1983).

two principles: the Logos and Sophia. The Logos is a principle directed from God toward man while the principle of Sophia is directed from man toward God. The former (God's descent into the created world) is a theurgic act, and the latter (man's ascent to the spheres of heaven and becoming part of the divine) is a sophiurgic act. These two principles meet and unite in the Son of Mary, Jesus Christ.[8]

Bulgakov created a unique type of sophiology, a new monistic system. Sophia, for him, is universal being, both human and divine. She is Ousia, the essence, the essence of both God and the world. She is a divine nature who is not a person but became a person in three persons. However, this does not imply the existence of four persons or a quaternity, because the only divine essence is embodied by the three persons.[9] At the same time Sophia constitutes the framework of nature, which is embodied by created beings. The latter is the panorganism of ideas.

Bulgakov argues that Ousia-Sophia is not a hypostasis (person), but an essence. It is nature that receives form in different hypostases, and divine and human relationships and thereby becomes existential, specific, and unique. The divine and created nature of Sophia is comprised of unity and difference. It is an antinomy, a secret. This solution might lead some to suspect Bulgakov of pantheism (and it did). Although Bulgakov clearly sees the differences between each level, he emphasizes that the root of the unity of being is the good nature of the world (based on Gen 1:31). Everything has a divine nature since "you will be as gods" (Gen 3:5).

It might seem a weakness of this theory that most sophiologists regard Sophia as a personal reality. Bulgakov holds that she is an ontological principle, the entelechy of the world, the finality and actualizing force of the universe. She is the World-Soul. He holds that she is androgynous; she is a man and a woman at the same time. She is polar. She is the dialectical representation of the Logos and the soul. She is the harmonious unity of animus-anima, *raison et coeur.*

8. Hajnády, *Sophia*, 255.
9. After all, it does have a precedent: Meister Eckhart, who made a difference between God and the three persons in the same way.

Like his contemporaries, Bulgakov accepts Mary as the incarnation of Sophia, but he has a cosmological view of this principle. Mary is the mother of mankind. She is universal humanity, the spiritual source of creation and the mother and heart of the world. He knows her intimate relationship with the Holy Spirit; when the Holy Spirit descended, he enabled Mary to become the mother of God. Similar to a number of his predecessors, Bulgakov lists the following among Sophia's attributes: she is the daughter of the Father, the bride and mother of the Sun, the human image and icon of the Holy Spirit. She is the heart and mother of the Church, the queen of the heavens, and the mother and bride of the Lamb.

Sophia in Russian Iconography and Church Architecture

The principle of *lex orandi, lex credendi* may be applied to church architecture and iconography. Indeed, churches and icons have played a dominant role in the communication of divine wisdom for the Russians of Kiev. The Church of Sophia was the center of cultural identity. It was the representation of beauty, social justice, and morality for all eternity. The Russians often consecrated their churches to Sophia, the Divina Sapientia,[10] in their three capitals (Kiev, Polosk, and Novgorod) and later in other cities as well. The churches of Uspensky and Blagoveschensky were originally dedicated to Sophia. Only later were they renamed according to certain notions of the Divine Mother. Orthodox believers hold that the embodied idea of God signified in the world cannot be expressed more effectively than it is expressed by the Cathedral of Sophia in Kiev, which is referred to as the "mother of all the churches in Russia."[11]

Regarding the icons, Sophia is represented in three different ways in Russian iconology: as an angel, as the Church, and as Mary. If she is an angel, she is represented in a form preceding her incarnation. Below her there is Mary with the child. In many cases she is the Angel of Good Advice, as, for example, on the Icon of the Holy Trin-

10. The Slavic people even named a capital after her: Sophia.
11. Hajnády, *Sophia*, 248.

ity[12] from the 19th century where Mary is the human icon of Sophia and Sophia represents the Holy Spirit. In the pictures depicting the Church there is a semi-circle with seven rays under the full circle of Christ, which is also a representation of Sophia before her incarnation. In the third type, Sophia is the great Orante, the Mother of God, as, for instance, in the Cathedral of Kiev, the Hermitage of Optina, and the Sion Cathedral of Tiflis where Sophia is represented as Mary. Florensky holds that Sophia should be interpreted as more than just the Logos even in the churches of Byzantium (Hagia Sophia, built by Constantine the Great, Hagia Eirene, and Hagia Dynamis). But even if Sophia were no more than the guardian angel of the world, we should still regard her as significant to the future of the world.[13]

The depiction of the archangel could open up a path to the interpretation of Sophia as a divine person. Ancient Greek and Russian icons depict all three divine persons as angels based on Genesis 18:1–15.[14] In the famous Holy Trinity icon[15] of Andrei Rublev (1360–1430) we can see the Father, the Son, and the Holy Spirit from left to right. In the Holy Trinity icon of Theophanes the Greek[16] in the Church of Novgorod, consecrated to the Transfiguration of our Lord in 1378, the angel in the middle spreads its wings above the other two angels next to it.[17] This act emphasizes the priority of the Father. We should compare this approach to the picture of the Holy Trinity in Urschalling where the person in the middle is the Holy Spirit represented by the figure of a woman.[18] It is true that this could change the usual order of persons, but the Greek and Slavic traditions do not point in that direction.

---

12. See Appendix XII.

13. Schipflinger, *Sophia*, 188.

14. István Ivancsó, "Holy Trinity," in *Icon and Liturgy*, 20 (Nyíregyháza: Saint Athanase Greek Catholic College of Theology, 2002).

15. See appendix XIII. Rublev emphasizes the equality and unity of the three persons.

16. See Appendix XIV.

17. The special position of the angel in the middle was pointed out in Hungary by Zoltan Kadar, *Fine Arts Review* (1999): 188–89.

18. See Appendix XVIII.

Sophiology in Russian Religious Philosophy

Let us have a look at a few important details concerning the representations of Divine Wisdom. In the Sophia icon of Novgorod,[19] on the basis of which the Novgorod type of icons were created, there is the queen-like figure of the Virgin Sophia in the middle with wings (angel), the bride of the Logos; the Word, who is standing above her, is represented by the figure of Christ with a sign saying "*Ho On*," which means divine. Sophia is an angel with Mary on her right. Mary is her embodiment with the baby Jesus on her heart. On her left is John the Baptist. It is by no means a Christosophical representation, because Christ is represented as a separate individual in the picture. The Russian people regard the pre-incarnation of Sophia as a person embodied by Mary. This form of representation had an influence on Western spirituality and it is still important from the point of view of ecumenism.[20]

Stroganov's icon *Sophia as a Bride and her Wedding* was created around 1600.[21] Its theme is "The bride is on the right." There is an angel in the middle between Mary and John the Baptist. Above them is the Father with angels and a sign: "Psalm 45." According to traditional interpretation, it is an icon of *deisis* (the hierarchy of intermediaries). There is Sophia in the middle, who is identical with Christ. Left of him/her there is Mary and on the right and the Baptist in an orante gesture. But something is wrong here. Why would Sophia be represented as a woman?

Well, Sophia is not Christ but a person different from him. In fact here we are dealing with a wedding icon. In the words of the Old Testament it is the wedding of Yahweh and Hakmoth-Sophia. The figure of Solomon indicates that he was the one who announced this wedding. In the words of the New Testament, it is the wedding of Jesus Christ and his mother/bride (Mary and/or the Church). The great messenger who heralded the wedding is John the Baptist, for it is the wedding of the Lamb that is taking place now. At the side there are Joachim and Anna, the parents of Mary, who are the human instruments of the incarnation of Sophia.

19. See Appendix XV.
20. Schipflinger, *Sophia*, 195.
21. See Appendix XVI.

In the Cathedral of Saint Sophia Kiev[22] Sophia stands behind the icons as Orante in a blue and golden dress with the sign *Mether Theou* (The Mother of God). She is the heavenly Sophia who became human in Mary. Her arms are open because she is awaiting the Logos. That is what she is praying for, and she is ready to help him become human to save the human race.

In the icon Mary is represented with the child and Christ with the book. Mary is Wisdom become human, the Divine Mother with the child in her lap. The book in the hands of Christ is the Torah, the intellectual framework of Wisdom and the universe. Consequently, Sophia is the individualization of the Torah and the universe. If Mary carries Christ, Christ carries the incarnation of Wisdom: Mary. In other words, what we see are three different manifestations of Sophia.[23] At the top there is the heavenly Sophia-Mary in a human form with the Logos delivered by her. On the right there is Christ with the book in his hand: it is the good news of the incarnated Logos to the world. Sophia is the bride and beloved colleague of Christ in the work of redemption. The Russian soul has left behind a very rich heritage of sophiology in its icons and churches.

22. See Appendix XVII.
23. Schipflinger, *Sophia*, 195.

13

Carl Gustav Jung
on the Witness Stand

B ESIDES theologians, mystics, and scientists, at least one modern psychologist, Carl Gustav Jung, has also made a statement
about sophiology. So we can call Jung to the witness stand. In
his work, *Psychology and Religion: West and East*, he writes again
and again about the form of Sophia, and he makes the case that the
feminine principle is present in the sources of Christianity and its
system.[1] Clearly speaking, he has his own sophiology, but not a
theological or existential one. Rather, his is a psychological sophiology.

Jung outstandingly makes an attempt to trace the genesis of the
biblical Sophia. He marks four main sources: the Old Testament's
wisdom literature, Hellenism, Hinduism, and Gnosticism. One of
his biblical examples is Proverbs, particularly Proverbs 8:22–31. Jung
sees these verses as conclusive, so much the more because these are
not only canonically·Catholic, but included in both the Jewish and
Protestant canons as well.

Jung explains his understanding of this sophiological core-text:
"This Sophia, who already shares certain essential qualities with the
Johannine Logos, is on the one hand closely associated with the
Hebrew Chochma, but on the other hand goes so far beyond it that
one can hardly fail to think of the Indian Shakti.[2] Nothing else, but

---

1. Carl Gustav Jung, *Psychology and Religion: West and East*, vol. 11 of *The Col-
lected Works of C. G. Jung*, trans. R. F. C. Hull (Pantheon, New York, 1958).
2. *Amon Jahveh*, in the role of God's favorite and lover (Prov 8:30).

the impersonated productive divine energy."[3] At this point he immediately refers to his new supposition, the Sophia concept's deeper source: "Relations with India certainly existed at that time [the time of the Ptolemys]."

Another biblical source about wisdom in Jung's insight is the Book of Sirach (Ecclesiasticus) written around 200 BC.[4] He quotes it in full form, and it is worth recalling another key sophiological source, thinking about the text as the self-confession of Wisdom, and even as an inner dialogue between Jahve and Sophia, as, for example, in the prologue of John's Gospel concerning the Father and the Logos. The whole 24th chapter of Sirach tells us the same:

 1 "Wisdom shall praise herself, and shall glory in the midst of her people.
 2 In the congregation of the most High shall she open her mouth, and triumph before his power.
 3 I came out of the mouth of the most High, and covered the earth as a cloud.
 4 I dwelt in high places, and my throne is in a cloudy pillar.
 5 I alone compassed the circuit of heaven, and walked in the bottom of the deep.
 6 In the waves of the sea and in all the earth, and in every people and nation, I got a possession.
 7 With all these I sought rest: and in whose inheritance shall I abide?
 8 So the Creator of all things gave me a commandment, and he that made me caused my tabernacle to rest, and said, Let thy dwelling be in Jacob, and thine inheritance in Israel.
 9 He created me from the beginning before the world, and I shall never fail.
 10 In the holy tabernacle I served before him; and so was I established in Sion.
 11 Likewise in the beloved city he gave me rest, and in Jerusalem was my power.
 12 And I took root in an honorable people, even in the portion of the Lord's inheritance.

3. Jung, *Psychology and Religion*, 387.
4. Ibid.

13 I was exalted like a cedar in Libanus, and as a cypress tree upon the mountains of Hermon.

14 I was exalted like a palm tree in Engaddi, and as a rose plant in Jericho, as a fair olive tree in a pleasant field, and grew up as a plane tree by the water.

15 I gave a sweet smell like cinnamon and aspalathus, and I yielded a pleasant odor like the best myrrh, as galbanum, and onyx, and sweet storax, and as the fume of frankincense in the tabernacle.

16 As the turpentine tree I stretched out my branches, and my branches are the branches of honor and grace.

17 As the vine brought I forth pleasant savor, and my flowers are the fruit of honor and riches.

18 I am the mother of fair love, and fear, and knowledge, and holy hope: I therefore, being eternal, am given to all my children which are named of him.

19 Come unto me, all ye that be desirous of me, and fill yourselves with my fruits.

20 For my memorial is sweeter than honey, and mine inheritance than the honeycomb.

21 They that eat me shall yet be hungry, and they that drink me shall yet be thirsty.

22 He that obeyeth me shall never be confounded, and they that work by me shall not do amiss."

Jung not only cites the text, but also makes a profound psychological analysis: "It is worthwhile to examine this text more closely. Wisdom describes herself, in effect, as the Logos, the Word of God."[5] To that extent, Jung considers the method of the New Testament or patrology as it applies the idea of *Wisdom* (or one of its forms) to the term *Logos*: "She corresponds in almost every feature to the Logos of St. John."[6] Nevertheless, Jung connects the concept of Wisdom not only to the Logos, but also to God's Spirit; he notices the internal bond between *Hokmah* and *Ruach* (Wisdom and Spirit): "As *Ruach*, the spirit of God, she brooded over the waters of the beginning (Gen 1:2)."[7]

5. Jung, *Psychology and Religion*, 388.
6. Ibid.
7. Ibid.

Jung wonderfully summarizes the possibilities of the Hokmah-Sophia concept, in light of his own psychological and religious historical parallels: "She is the feminine numen of the 'metropolis' par excellence, of Jerusalem the mother-city. She is the mother-beloved, a reflection of Ishtar, the pagan city-goddess. This is confirmed by the detailed comparison of Wisdom with trees, such as the cedar, palm, terebinth ('turpentine-tree'), olive, cypress, etc. All these trees have from ancient times been symbols of the Semitic love- and mother-goddess."[8] He delightfully describes the symbols of nature associated with Wisdom: "A holy tree always stood beside her [Hokmah's] altar on high places. In the Old Testament oaks and terebinths are oracle trees. God or angels are said to appear in or beside trees. David consulted a mulberry-tree oracle."[9]

Jung does not procrastinate, and in no time arrives at his religious parallels—"The tree in Babylon represented Tammuz, the son-lover, just as it represented Osiris, Adonis, Attis, and Dionysus, the young dying gods of the Near East"—and immediately gives us analogies from the Old Testament:

All these symbolic attributes also occur in the Song of Songs, as characteristics of the *sponsus* as well as the *sponsa*. The vine, the grape, the vine flower, and the vineyard play a significant role here. The Beloved is like an apple tree; she shall come down from the mountains (the cult places of the mother-goddess), "from the lions' dens, from the mountains of the leopards"; her womb is "an orchard of pomegranates, with pleasant fruits, camphire with spikenard, spikenard and saffron, calamus and cinnamon, with all trees of frankincense, myrrh and aloes, with all the chief spices." Her hands "dropped with myrrh." [Jung immediately adds:] (Adonis, we may remember, was born of the myrrh).[10]

With all these he clearly demonstrates Sophia's womanhood.

He also keeps the fulfillment of the wisdom literature (particularly the Book of Wisdom) in mind: "The pneumatic nature of Sophia as well as her world-building Maya character come out still

8. Ibid.
9. Ibid.
10. Jung, *Psychology and Religion*, 388.

more clearly in the apocryphal Wisdom of Solomon." He highlights these basic features: "wisdom is a loving spirit" and "kind to man" (Wisdom 1:6 and 7:23). She is "the worker of all things," "in her is an understanding spirit, holy." She is "the breath of the power of God," "a pure effluence flowing from the glory of the Almighty," "the brightness of the everlasting light, the unspotted mirror of the power of God" and being "most subtil," who "passeth and goeth through all things by reason of her pureness" (7:22–26). She is "conversant with God" and "the Lord of all things himself loved her" (8:3). "Who of all that are is a more cunning workman than she?" (8:6). She is sent from heaven and from the throne of glory as a "Holy Spirit" (9:10 and 17). "As a psychopomp she leads the way to God and assures immortality"[11] (6:18 and 8:13). He also recognizes that Sophia foreshadows the Holy Spirit as Comforter: "Like the Holy Spirit, Wisdom is given as a gift to the elect, an idea that is taken up again in the doctrine of the Paraclete."[12]

It is unequivocal to Jung to combine the concept of Jahve of the Hokmah and the *Ruach*, the Spirit's maternal-feminine character. He points out, however, that, unfortunately, this Sophia-concept has not become widespread among the people of the Old Testament. According to Jung, it is clearly shown that "Job obviously does not know enough about the Sophia who is coeternal with God. . . . One misses Sophia's 'love of mankind' more than ever. Even Job longs for the Wisdom which is nowhere to be found."[13]

According to Jung, Job's case also shows that the faithful's perception moved in two directions at the final period of the Old Testament. There were those who never recognized the concept of Wisdom. This lack of comprehension is interpreted by Jung: "Yahweh had lost sight of his pleromatic coexistence with Sophia since the days of the Creation. Her place was taken by the covenant with the chosen people, who were thus forced into the feminine role"— Israel, that is, had become God's bride in place of Sophia. For Jung, this trend psychologically means that "God's marriage with Israel

11. Ibid., 389.
12. Ibid.
13. Ibid., 396.

was therefore an essentially masculine affair, something like the founding of the Greek *polis*, which occurred about the same time. The inferiority of women was a settled fact.... Perfection is a masculine desideratum, while woman inclines by nature to completeness."[14]

The other, so to say, "sophiological way" to interpret Wisdom literature was to be aware of the newest developments of the Sophia-concept. At the latest period before Christ, this concept meant going beyond the Torah and the law, and it is worth quoting in greater detail how a perspective of profound religious transformation arose around the notion of Sophia-*Ruach*:

> Thus it was the men of the last few centuries before Christ who, at the gentle touch of the pre-existent Sophia, compensate Yahweh and his attitude, and at the same time complete *the anamnesis of Wisdom*. Taking a highly personified form that is clear proof of her autonomy, Wisdom reveals herself to men as a friendly helper and advocate against Yahweh, and shows them the bright side, the kind, just, and amiable aspect of their God.[15]

Jung clearly sees that Sophia—although she is descended from Yahweh—is, however, an autonomous person, a complementary theorem beside Yahweh, a counter-pole of God's authority. Jung sees the turn, attached to Hokmah as

> the reappearance of Sophia in the heavenly regions points to a coming act of creation. She is indeed the "master workman"; she realizes God's thoughts by clothing them in material form, which is the prerogative of all feminine beings. Her coexistence with Yahweh signifies the perpetual *hieros gamos* from which worlds are begotten and born. A momentous change is imminent: God desires to regenerate himself in the mystery of the heavenly nuptials—as, the chief gods of Egypt had done from time immemorial and to become man.[16]

For Jung the consequence of this turn is the incarnation of the Logos which, according to even the first Creeds, will happen by the

14. Ibid., 395.
15. Ibid., 396.
16. Ibid., 397.

Holy Spirit and of *Virgin Mary*. Here Jung comes to the Hokmah-theory's mariological dimension:

> The approach of Sophia betokens a new creation. But this time it is not the world that is to be changed; rather it is God who intends to change his own nature. Mankind is not, as before, to be destroyed, but saved. In this decision we can discern the "philanthropic" influence of Sophia: no new human beings are to be created, but only one, the God-man. For this purpose a contrary procedure must be employed. The Second Adam shall not, like the first, proceed directly from the hand of the Creator, but shall be born of a human woman. So this time priority falls to the Second Eve, not only in a temporal sense but in a material sense as well. On the basis of the so-called Proto-Evangelium, the Second Eve corresponds to "the woman and her seed" mentioned in Genesis 3:15, which shall bruise the serpent's head. . . . Thus Mary, the virgin, is chosen as the pure vessel for the coming birth of God.[17]

Jung states that this process takes place in the New Testament. He looks into the inner life of the Old Testament God and writes down the steps to Holy Trinity:

> As history draws nearer to the beginning of our era, the gods become more and more abstract and spiritualized. Even Yahweh had to submit to this transformation. In the Alexandrian philosophy that arose in the last century B.C., we witness not only an alteration of his nature but an emergence of two other divinities in his immediate vicinity: the Logos and Sophia. Together with him they form a triad, and this is a clear prefiguration of the post-Christian Trinity.[18]

As we know, on the theological field, Christ's dual nature and the mystery of the Trinity were closely intertwined in the polemics of the first centuries and they remained problematic. Jung wants to grab this mystery by a psychological base:

> The homoousia, whose general recognition was the cause of so many controversies, is absolutely necessary from a psychological standpoint, because . . . [t]he homoousia together with the *filioque*

17. Ibid., 398.
18. Ibid., 128.

assert that Christ and the Holy Spirit are both of the same substance as the Father. But since, psychologically, Christ must be understood as a symbol of the self,[19] and the descent of the Holy Spirit as the self's actualization in man, it follows that the self must represent something that is of the substance of the Father too.[20]

Jung holds the concept of *perichoresis* (the interoperability of divine persons) psychologically decisive:

> Interpenetrations of qualities and contents are typical not only of symbols in general, but also of the essential similarity of the contents symbolized. Without this similarity no interpenetration would be possible at all. We therefore find interpenetration also in the Christian conception of the Trinity, where the Father appears in the Son, the Son in the Father, the Holy Spirit in Father and Son, or both these in the Holy Spirit as the Paraclete. The progression from Father to Son and the Son's appearance on earth at a particular moment would represent the time element, while the spatial element would be personified by the *Mater Dei*. The mother quality was originally an attribute of the Holy Spirit, and the latter was known as Sophia-Sapientia by certain early Christians.[21]

We should set aside the mariology now. It is conclusive that Jung holds to, according to the early Christian view, the Holy Spirit's motherly nature. As a source he refers to the Acts of Thomas, where the believers turn to the Holy Spirit as to a mother:[22] "This feminine quality could not be completely eradicated; it still adheres to the symbol of the Holy Spirit, the *columba Spiritus Sancti*."[23]

Jung sees the continuation of Sophia's philanthropic role in Jesus's humaneness and also in Mary's intercession: "With regard to the human side of Christ, if we can speak of a 'purely human' aspect at all, what stands out particularly clearly is his love of mankind.

---

19. The self (*selbst*) is Jung's basic term for our human innermost core, ourselves.

20. Ibid., 194.

21. Ibid., 73.

22. H. Hennecke, *Neutestamentliche Apokryphen* (Berlin: Mohr, 1987), 266. Sophia represents the Holy Spirit.

23. The Holy Spirit as mother-dove. Jung, *Psychology and Religion*, 73.

This feature is already implied in the relationship of Mary to Sophia, and especially in his genesis by the Holy Spirit, whose feminine nature is personified by Sophia," adding that, "since she is the preliminary historical form of the *pneuma hagion*, who is symbolized by the dove, the bird belonging to the love-goddess."[24]

Jung reckons there to be a straight path from Sophia's form to the Virgin Mary:

> The divine immaculateness of her status makes it immediately clear that she not only bears the image of God (*imago Dei*) in undiminished purity, but, as the bride of God, is also the incarnation of her prototype, namely Sophia. Her love of mankind, widely emphasized in the ancient writings, suggests that in this newest creation of his Yahweh has allowed himself to be extensively influenced by Sophia. For Mary, the blessed among women, is a friend and intercessor for sinners, which all men are.[25]

She is *en bloc* identical with Sophia.

Jung's evidence that Mary is the embodied Sophia, is the *epiteton ornans* from the Litany of Loreto, the *sedes sapientiae,* which clearly refers to Mary and reminds us that the Catholic Church has taken Mary's readings from the Wisdom books. It tells us that Sophia's form directs us to Mary's role in salvation.

There is another component of Jung's sophiology that suggests that the Spirit's slightly feminine character could be influenced by Gnosticism, which was full of theories about Sophia. As he observes of the Gnostic idea of Sophia and the Sapientia figure of the medieval natural philosophers,

> who said of her: *In gremio matris sedet sapientia patris* (the wisdom of the father lies in the lap of the mother). These psychological relationships do something to explain why the Holy Spirit was interpreted as the mother, but they add nothing to our understanding of the Holy Spirit as such, because it is impossible to see how the mother could come third when her natural place would be second.[26]

24. Ibid., 407.
25. Ibid., 398.
26. Ibid., 162.

It is as if Jung also explains here the standstill of this promising sophiology.

Nevertheless, the Gnostic influence also feeds Jung to form his quaternity theories about Mary, as Mary takes a divine place as a fourth next to the Holy Trinity: "The Gnostic interpretation of the Holy Spirit as the Mother contains a core of truth in that Mary was the instrument of God's birth and so became involved in the trinitarian drama as a human being. The Mother of God can, therefore, be regarded as a symbol of mankind's essential participation in the Trinity."[27] Naturally, we cannot take these conclusions seriously from a theological point-of-view.

In his own mariology, Jung considers the proof of the quaternity theory in modern Catholic statements regarding the Immaculate Conception and Assumption, or regarding Mary's role, albeit unrecognized, as Co-Redeemer, stating in this connection:

> Like Sophia, she is a mediatrix who leads the way to God and assures man of immortality. Her Assumption is therefore the prototype of man's bodily resurrection. As the bride of God and Queen of Heaven she holds the place of the Old Testament Sophia.[28]

He goes even further. In fact, Jung interprets the dogmas audaciously:

> Remarkable indeed are the unusual precautions which surround the making of Mary: immaculate conception, extirpation of the taint of sin, everlasting virginity. . . . By having these special measures applied to her, Mary is elevated to the status of a goddess and consequently loses something of her humanity: she will not conceive her child in sin, like all other mothers, and therefore he also will never be a human being, but a god.[29]

Of course, *I do not agree* with these conclusions, neither do any professional theologians, because, to cite only the Byzantine Catholic Liturgy, it is clear that we pray for Mary just as for all of us: "*in*

27. Ibid., 161.
28. Ibid., 398.
29. Ibid., 399.

behalf of all and for all." Neither Christians of the East nor of the West have ever regarded her as a deity.

We must go beyond this argument. For Jung, the most significant sophiological source is the Book of Revelation. As he writes of the text:

> after the destruction of Jerusalem, a vision of the sun-woman, "with the moon under her feet, and on her head a crown of twelve stars." She was in the pangs of birth, and before her stood a great red dragon that wanted to devour her child. This vision is altogether out of context. . . . [O]ne feels that this image is original. . . . The vision is introduced by the opening of the temple in heaven and the sight of the Ark of the Covenant. This is probably a prelude to the descent of the heavenly bride, Jerusalem, an equivalent of Sophia, for it is all part of the heavenly *hieros gamos*, whose fruit is a divine man-child. He is threatened with the fate of Apollo, the son of Leto, who was likewise pursued by a dragon. But here we must dwell for a moment on the figure of the mother. She is "a woman clothed with the sun."

Who is she? Jung answers that

> another possible model to be considered is the *cosmic Sophia*, to whom John refers on more than one occasion. She could easily be taken as the mother of the divine child (the son would then correspond to the *filius sapientiae* of medieval alchemy), since she is obviously a woman in heaven, i.e., a goddess or consort of a god. Sophia comes up to this definition, and so does the transfigured Mary.[30]

With his psychoanalytic apparatus, Jung starts to extrapolate on the woman clothed with the sun and the reborn Son:

> Strangely, suddenly, as if it did not belong there, the sun-woman with her child appears in the stream of apocalyptic visions. He belongs to another, future world. . . . Therefore the Apocalypse closes, like the classical individuation process, with the symbol of *the hieros gamos*, the marriage of the son with the mother-bride. But the marriage takes place in heaven, where "nothing unclean" enters, high above the devastated world. Light consorts with

---

30. Ibid., 442.

light. . . . Only in the last days will the vision of the sun-woman be fulfilled.[31]

Jung believes that this symbolic system betokens "the Old Testament anamnesis of Sophia. The nuptial union in the *thalamus* (bridal-chamber) signifies the *hieros gamos* . . . [and this] means the desire for the birth of a savior, a peacemaker, a *'mediator pacem faciens inter inimicos,'* [a mediator making peace between enemies]. Although he is already born in the pleroma, his birth in time can only be accomplished when it is perceived, recognized, and declared by man." He adds, with some disappointment, that there is a "failure to understand that God has eternally wanted to become man, and for that purpose continually incarnates through the Holy Spirit in the temporal sphere."[32]

So Jung sees in the Book of Revelation that the Son's birth is the culmination of a process that was foretold in the Old Testament form of Sophia:

> Ever since John the apocalyptist experienced for the first time (perhaps unconsciously) that conflict into which Christianity inevitably leads, mankind has groaned under this burden: God wanted to become man, and still wants to. That is probably why John experienced in his vision a second birth of a son from the mother Sophia, a divine birth . . . which anticipated the *filius sapientiae*, the essence of the individuation process.[33]

Jung finds the realization of his own central concept, *individuation*, in this birth: "That higher and 'complete' (*teleios*) man is begotten by the 'unknown' father and born from Wisdom, and it is he who, in the figure of the *puer aeternus*—'*vultu mutabilis albus et ater*'[34]—represents our totality, which transcends consciousness." At this point, theology prefers speaking about salvation, transformation, theosis.

To the closing picture of Revelation Jung appends this interpretation:

31. Ibid., 458.
32. Ibid., 463.
33. Ibid., 455.
34. Of changeful countenance, both white and black.

This final vision, which is generally interpreted as referring to the relationship of Christ to his Church, has the meaning of a "uniting symbol" and is therefore a representation of perfection and wholeness.... Heaven is masculine, but the earth is feminine. Therefore God has his throne in heaven, while Wisdom has hers on the earth, as she says in Ecclesiasticus: "Likewise in the beloved city he gave me rest, and in Jerusalem was my power." She (Sophia) is the "mother of fair love," and when John pictures Jerusalem as the bride he is probably following Ecclesiasticus. The city is Sophia, who was with God before time began, and at the end of time will be reunited with God through the sacred marriage. As a feminine being she coincides with the earth, from which, so a Church Father tells us, Christ was born.[35]

Jung concludes that the Virgin Mary entered the divine sphere as the fourth. He also detects this in the dogma of the Assumptio Mariae, because with this "Mary as the bride is united with the son in the heavenly bridal chamber, and, as Sophia, with the Godhead."[36] He even cites the dogma as proof: "The place of the bride whom the Father had espoused was in the heavenly courts." He also remarks that even St. John Damascene pointed out the similarity between the bride of the Song of Songs and Mary, as did St. Anthony of Padua, who wrote: "so in like manner arose the Ark which he had sanctified, when on this day the Virgin Mother was taken up to her heavenly bridal-chamber."[37] Jung is also quite inspired by the idea of Mary's bodily assumption: "It is psychologically significant for our day that in the year 1950 the heavenly bride was united with the bridegroom. In order to interpret this event, one has to consider not only the arguments adduced by the Papal Bull, but the prefigurations in the apocalyptic marriage of the Lamb."[38]

These secrets could be easily answered without regarding Mary as a member of some godly quaternity. It seems quite illogical, that this Jung who, in essence, endorses a feminine interpretation of the Holy Spirit would then wish to apply another feminine existence into the

35. Ibid., 448.
36. Ibid., 458.
37. Ibid.
38. Ibid., 462.

godly sphere. The 2000-year-old faith holds Mary as a creature; her assumption can easily and satisfactorily be explained by salvation.

To sum up, Carl Gustav Jung enriched modern sophiology on numerous points, even if his viewpoint was entirely psychological. He strengthened the bond and continuity between the concepts of Sophia and the Holy Spirit and strongly represented that both the feminine element and the *hieros gamos* can be found even within the godly existence. The hymn of being resounds in his psychology.

14

The Many-Faced Sophia

N OW THAT we have reviewed the impact and implications of the teaching of scripture concerning Sophia, we can ascertain how this teaching has been increasingly clarified over the centuries. As the Lord Jesus declared, the Spirit "will guide you into all truth" (John 16:13). This process of clarification took place not only through forums like synods or papal encyclicals, which the Catholic Church designates as official, but also through the representatives of liturgy, iconography, and mysticism which also reached new insights. A term used in Eastern theology, *sobornosti*, or the consensus of the congregation, was at work in this clarification. The concept of Sophia revealed in the Old Testament became more and more profound, new shades of color were added, and this calls for a reinterpretation of the original theorems. First, we will raise the question whether Hokmah-Sophia can be viewed as a personal reality; second, whether we can find further points to secure the concept of Sophia in the New Testament; and third, we will investigate on what grounds we might be able to discover the feminine side of divine being.

Hokmah-Sophia:
Person or Personification?

The concept of Hokmah-Sophia-Wisdom was revealed in the wisdom books and their reception. Does this concept merely personify one of the features of God, His wisdom, or is it an independent hypostasis, a real person? First we have to clarify certain basic principles: what do we mean by personification; what is hypostasis;

what is a person;[1] and what do we mean by "Old Testament" in this context?

The meaning of personification in literature is different from personification in the history of religions. In literature, personification is a kind of allegory as in the expressions "Sun-God" or "Mother Earth." In the history of religions, personification is used as a device to represent certain features of God or the gods, like understanding, free will, daughter of wisdom, or as a device to represent the cosmic world order (as in World-Soul) or abstract concepts like agreement, fertility, love (viz. Concordia, Ceres, Amor).

The concept of hypostasis can also refer to two different meanings: one in the context of the history of religions and another in theology. In the history of religions, a relatively independent divine being appears as a feature, an action, or a role of a higher god, as, for example, the Egyptian Maat. In Jewish tradition such a hypostasis is Shekinah, the presence of God. In a theological context, hypostasis is equivalent to personality.

Yet what we do mean by person? A person is an individual being with his incommunicable peculiarity (like this man, Peter), who is endowed with intellect, free will, and independence. This individual being, person, Peter, is a grammatical subject (*suppositum*), the agent of an action. Only beings with an independent spiritual substance (either with or without a body) can be viewed as persons: and such are men, angels, and God.

The term "Old Testament" can also refer to different concepts. What it is for Christians is the *Tenach* or written teachings for Jews and it includes the laws of Moses and the prophets along with other books, but this compilation is different from the canon of the Old Testament of the early Church because it excludes books written in Greek (viz. the Septuagint). The exegesis of the Jewish compilation is comprised of the Talmud and the Kabbalah, which do not apply to Christian teaching. Christian scholars treat interpretations of the Old Testament as a covenant borrowed from Jewish scholarship separately from Christian aspects.

---

1. "Zu den Begriffen Personifikation, Hypostase und Person," in *Wörterbuch der Religionen*, ed. Adolf Bertholet (Stuttgart: Klett, 1976), 269.

The Many-Faced Sophia

Based on this approach, the term "Old Testament" refers to three different frameworks of reference: a purely Jewish, pre-Christian interpretation, which, naturally, cannot rely on Christian theology; a minimalist Christian interpretation, which ultimately is identical with the former in as much as it reflects on texts of the Old Testament by focusing on monotheism; and an expanded Christian interpretation, which makes references to the New Testament and to other Christian parallels and sees the first covenant or the Old Testament as a prophetic foreshadowing of the new covenant or the New Testament; and, finally, this latter interpretation includes later achievements of Christian scholarship.

Applying all that has been said to the topic of Sophia, the third interpretation results in various further differences. The early Church Fathers, for example, identify Sophia as Logos because they place the embodiment of God in the center and ignore a number of cosmological, theological, mariological, and eschatological features of Sophia that only came to light relatively recently.

As far as personality is concerned, the literature of wisdom often gives a voice to the mouth of Wisdom and occasionally she has the role of a speaker or a preacher. In Proverbs, for example, she is shouting in streets and squares. Much research was devoted to this aspect, but representatives of the Jewish and the minimalist Christian interpretation see it only as a poetic device because they will not tolerate a new person on the plane of divine being, and Hokmah-Sophia, for them, is merely a feature of God.[2]

Even such principle works as *Christ in der Welt* or the *Handbuch theologischer Grundbegriffe* and the *Bibellexikon*, and recent translations of scripture are limited in the same way, considering personification only from the historical aspect, or even going as far as claiming that expressions through personification are part of God's teaching.

The minimalist Christian interpretation only accepts the *personality* of Wisdom to the extent that she is equated with Logos. Arnold Strobl lists those Church Fathers who, exclusively in this sense, considered Hokmah-Sophia as an independent being, a person: St.

---

2. *Echte Bibel*, Bd. 4 (Würzburg: Herder, 1959), 418, 568.

Gregory the Theologian, St. Ambrose, St. Augustine, St. Bernard, St. Bonaventura. Yet, Strobl's conclusion is that Sophia cannot be a person because then her opposite, Folly, should also be a person.[3] Strobl, however, ignores the fact that Folly appears only sporadically in the wisdom books, while Wisdom is a leitmotiv with many shades and colors and with a personal weight.

The difficulty results from the circumstance that, on the one hand, according to Jewish concepts, another divine person beside Yahweh seems absurd, and within Christian terms, on the other hand, Sophia may appear as the fourth divine person next to the Holy Trinity. This is why most theologians accept Sophia as a created being only.

A contemporary example of the minimalist Christian interpretation is the *Biblical Theological Dictionary*, which talks about "wisdom according to God" instead of divine Wisdom in order to avoid the consideration of Sophia as a divine person, and it claims that wisdom is the prophetic antecedent of the Son of God or the Word: "The Son is the wisdom of the Father. This personal wisdom had been hidden in God, although it governed the universe, directed history and, indirectly, appeared in the Law and in the teachings of wise men. Now it revealed itself in Jesus Christ. The wisdom books of the Old Testament attain their ultimate meaning in this sense."[4]

The most recent edition of *Dogmatic* published by Vigilia considers mariological aspects of Sophia erroneous and claims that the chance to experience wisdom with God, His Son, or His Spirit is open to everyone; Mary may only have been able to sense this experience in an extraordinary way, but she was not exclusively subject to the experience.[5] In other words, the handbook of dogma rules out any attributes of Sophia as a divine person.

Divine wisdom, then, from the point of view of Jewish or minimalist Christian exegesis, is only a characteristic trait of God or,

3. Arnold Strobl, "Die Weisheit Israels," in *Enzyklopädie der Christ in der Welt* (Aschaffenburg: Pattloch, 1967), 89.

4. *Biblikus Teológiai Szótár* [*Biblical Theological Dictionary*] (Rome: Dario Detti, 1974), 158.

5. *A dogmatika kézikönyve* [*A Handbook of Dogmatics*], vol. II (Budapest: Vigilia, 1996), 186.

according to the Christian concept, of Logos, or of the Holy Spirit. In this frame of mind, one can see wisdom as *arche*, the primal cause of creation, *entelechia*, or a personification of mankind, but not necessarily as a person. Yet, there could be a further sophiological minimum that may be acceptable to both Jewish and Christian thought: we could view Sophia as the divine essence (*ousia tou Theou, essentia Dei*). From a Christian perspective, each person of the Holy Trinity inherently bears Sophia; she becomes a person within them (*enhypostasiation*) and a quasi-fourth person is not needed: Sophia is personal only *within* the Trinity.[6] As we have seen, Bulgakov subscribed to this point of view.

This minimalist interpretation may go as far as considering the final *entelechia* a World-Soul (but still a created principle) as parallels of science and philosophy allude to the concept and especially as Teilhard de Chardin sees it: "the Universe is personal. If our greatest problem is to negotiate between universality and subjectivity, for Teilhard the two are not contradictory terms."[7] Solovyov approves this approach: "Sophia is not only an object of divine activity like the primal cosmos which includes all future concepts and ideas is; rather, she is, in effect, an animate being, a rational World-fund, a World-Soul [...], an ideal person representing the world and especially man [...], the universal and unique organism of all humankind. [...] In reality, she is the mother of man and of all beings."[8]

In this sense, Sophia may be viewed as a created person standing next to God like an angel since they share a throne (Wisdom 9:4). In scripture angels without bodies have an influence on the cosmos: God "makes his angels spirits; his ministers flaming fire" (Psalm 104:4). Archangels Michael and Gabriel are usually depicted with globes in their hands. In Christian iconography, Sophia as World-Soul is sometimes depicted as an angel. Our Lord Jesus designates malevolent spirits "the emperors of the World [cosmos]" (John 14:31); it seems, therefore, that even within the world of spirits a bipolarity exists: the poles of good and evil. A cosmic, rational, and

---

6. Schipflinger, *Sophia*, 223.
7. *Teilhard de Chardin-Lexikon*, vol. 2 (Freiburg: Herder, 1971), 244.
8. Karl Pfleger, *Die verwegene Christozentrik* (Freiburg: Herder, 1964), 86.

personal being with positive charge, Sophia should be accepted by both Jewish and Christian tradition.

But let us return to identifying Sophia as World-Soul. A further aspect of this equalization, already in line with a broad Christian interpretation, is that many scholars believe that Sophia was embodied in the Virgin Mary and/or in the Church. The hymns and Sophia churches of the Christian East, icons of Mary, and even some streams of thought in Western Christianity examine Sophia from a mariological or ecclesiological perspective. The feasts of Mary in Roman Catholic liturgy also seem to support this argument since texts of these feasts are taken from the literature of wisdom. (The liturgical reform changed some of the texts, but the original texts co-exist with these as options.)

Important testimonies of Sophia as a person are attested to by those canonized saints who regard her as their mother, their teacher, their leader, as Solomon regarded her his own mother. These include the apostle to the Slavs, St. Cyril, who devoted himself to Sophia as a young man; St. Hildegard of Bingen, whose visions we can only understand from a sophiological perspective; Heinrich Suso, who regards Sophia as his Lady in the way that knights of the Middle Ages regarded their ladies; and Saint Louis-Marie Grignion de Montfort.

In the broader Christian interpretation the idea whether we can consider Sophia as a divine person arose quite early: from the beginning of Christianity there were people who believed it was so. Among them are Origen, St. Athanasius, the Cappadocian Fathers, St. Augustine, and others such as those who equated Sophia with the Logos. There are, further, those early Syrian theologians and Irenaeus or Theophilus of Antioch, who equate her with the Holy Spirit. Beyond these saints and mystics, proof of the equation theory can be derived from texts of the liturgy and testimonies of iconography, which we have already encountered when we reviewed traditional approaches. The concept of non-created Sophia we are going to discuss below.

The two strands, that is, the logo-centric, which equates Sophia with Logos, and the sophiological, which regards Sophia as an independent person, complement each other since, as we have seen,

Logos and Sophia can be seen in a hierogamic relation. The Church Fathers understood the vision of Proverbs 8:30 to refer to the Logos, but a number of mystics understood it to refer to Sophia. The two together are bride and bridegroom.

Based on what has been said so far the following arguments seem to support considerations of Sophia as a person (for the time being we only focus on the Old Testament):

1. Scripture depicts Sophia as a spiritual being that has intellect, free will, and all the features, roles, and characteristics that a person has.

2. The literature of wisdom depicts her as a created, person-like female who is unlike God.

3. As far as her connection to God is concerned, she acts as a consultant of God, she is His partner in creation and she dances for Him.

4. As far as her relationship to the world is concerned, she upholds, directs, manages, and renews the world with intelligence, power, and benevolence.

5. She teaches and warns man as mother, as governess, as good wife.

6. The impersonal interpretation cannot be held because the books of wisdom describe her as a relatively independently acting being; therefore, she is at least a dynamic concept and a grammatical subject in the history of religion.

7. Christian tradition treats her from the beginning as a person and by identifying her with the Logos or the Holy Spirit connects her, not only allegorically, to Mary, to the Church, or to mankind and to creation.

8. Christian piety and devotional icons, hymns, and churches to Sophia.

9. Christian theologians, philosophers, mystics, and saints have regarded her as a person, conversed with her and, based on experience, described her as mother, as friend, as bride, as Lady, and they venerated her as such and called on others to do the same.

10. Contemporary sophiology expanded this view with cosmic dimensions, but this development does not exclude an interpretation of Sophia as a person; in fact, it requires it.

New Concepts in the New Testament

As we have seen, Christian thinking required a learning curve in its two-thousand-year history to accept with growing conviction the roles of Sophia and Logos side-by-side. The fact that texts are attributed to the "apostle to the pagans" that directly refer to elements in the literature of wisdom and these references allude to a contradiction, namely, to a *logo monist* point of view, can be easily discarded: places in the Old Testament refer to Sophia, while Paul refers to Christ.

Proverbs 8:24: When there were no depths, I was brought forth.

Colossians 1:17: He is before all things, and by Him all things consist.

Proverbs 8:22: The Lord possessed me in the beginning of his way, before his works of old.

Colossians 1:18: He is the beginning, in all things He might have the pre-eminence.

Wisdom 9:1: Thou created all with thy words and created man with thy wisdom.

Colossians 1:16: By Him were all things created that are in heaven, and that are in earth, all things were created by Him, and for Him.

Sirach 24:5: I came forth from among the lips of the Almighty as first-born before all else.

Colossians 1:15: [Christ] is the image of the invisible God, the first-born of every creature.

Wisdom 7:26: [Wisdom] is a reflection of God's perfection.

Wisdom 7:25, 26: The breath of God's power, the pouring forth of God's glory, a mirror of His perfection.

Hebrews 1:2–3: [By Christ] he made the world; who is the brightness of His glory, and the express image of His person, and upholds all things by the word of His power.

The Many-Faced Sophia

The question remains whether we treat the above places as parallels, identical references, or a double unity. From as early as the Church Fathers, many exegetes have seen the two sides as equal; in other words, they believe that the parallels show the equation of Logos and Sophia. But if we treat Sophia and Logos as bride and bridegroom, the similarities between the two may result from their similar role or function as well. As the perfect realization of the duality of man and woman, they together model the image of God. Moreover, the parallels confirm the possibility of seeing Sophia as a personal entity since this is the only way the two sides could become complementary. The promotion of Sophia's status to a personal entity does not lessen the significance of the ranks of trinitology.

The teaching of Paul on Sophia is extended by the Book of Revelation, which adds an eschatological dimension to Sophia as the Church: "Worthy is the Lamb that was slain to receive power and riches, wisdom and strength, honor and glory and blessing" (5:12). We can identify expressions pertaining to Christ and to His body (Sophia embodied and the devotion of the Church): power, strength, and glory are features of Christ, the embodied Son of God, while riches, the fruits of wisdom, honor, and blessing refer to the Church so that the Church as the embodied Sophia can honor and bless Christ. The excerpt becomes meaningful only in the context of the Pauline concept of the body of Christ.

And now we have arrived at an extraordinary detail which permeates the New Testament: the clearest theological expression of the divine nuptial, the wedding of the Lamb. The Lord Jesus revealed himself as a bridegroom (viz. Matt 9:15) and compared the word of God to a wedding (Matt 22:2 and 24:6). The first of his public appearances according to John was the marriage at Cana (John 2). John the Baptist also made a reference to this detail: "The one who has the bride is the bridegroom; the best man, who stands and listens to him, rejoices greatly at the bridegroom's voice. So this joy of mine has been made complete" (John 3:29). The term used by John became part of both Western and Eastern liturgies: Jesus is the Lamb of God (John 1:36).

The detail is completed by an eschatological element in Revelation; St. John here refers back to the invitation to the wedding:

"Blessed are those who have been called to the wedding feast of the Lamb" (19:9); "For the wedding day of the Lamb has come, his bride has made herself ready" (19:7); and "Come here. I will show you the bride, the wife of the Lamb" (21:9). On the basis of Logos-Sophia it is clear that the wife theologically is Sophia. Similarly to the literature of wisdom and the Kabbalah, the Book of Revelation also envisions Sophia as the new Jerusalem: "I also saw the holy city, a new Jerusalem, coming down out of heaven from God, prepared as a bride adorned for her husband" (21:2).

The theological interpretation reveals a mariological explanation as well, since Mary is the Mother of the Church. This mariological line is extended by Matthew and Luke in their history of the child, especially in the good news of Mary; in the theology of John the Baptist; in the wedding at Cana; Mary by the cross; the sun-adorned lady in Revelation; as well as in the news of Pentecost in the Acts of the Apostles. And here I would uphold Fr. Schipflinger's theory: the relationship between the Lord Jesus and his mother is not a *hieros gamos* relation; rather, it is another wonderful form of the meeting of man and woman, namely the connection of mother and son, which can easily be seen as the realization of the Sophia-principle as we have seen in the philosophical and historical parallels cited above.

Many features of Sophia in the Old Testament are realized in the figure of Mary: "Highly favored" (Luke 1:28, viz. Wisdom 7:26: "the spotless mirror of the power of God"); "the Lord is with thee" (Luke 1:28, viz. Wisdom 8:3: "she dwells with God"); she bears Christ: "Blessed is the womb that bare thee" (Luke 11:27); and according to her own testimony she is "the handmaid of the Lord" (Luke 1:38); and who followed the teaching of the literature of wisdom: "when you come to serve the Lord, prepare yourself for trials" (Sirach 2:1). As Hokmah and Shekinah, she identifies with Israel; in fact, she personifies it (viz. "Magnificat"). A whole line of mystics, the liturgy, and the iconography of the Eastern Church and the Marian devotion of Western Christianity (by taking readings from the literature of wisdom for feasts of the Virgin) all acknowledge alike that Mary is Sophia embodied and that all values of salvation accumulate in her as in a forerunner.

The Many-Faced Sophia

Logos in Arche

John's Prologue may raise the question again whether the text should be interpreted as pure logos monism. According to Schipflinger, at the end of verse 1, the expression: "the Word was God" only makes sense as a reference to Logos. Likewise, in verse 12: "to those who did accept him he gave power to become sons of God," and in verse 16: "From his fullness we have all received, grace in place of grace." Therefore, the redeeming-divinizing role of Logos and its being within the Holy Trinity and within God, for Schipflinger, seems apparent.[9]

However, certain passages of John's Prologue, like some Pauline texts, can be seen in parallel with details in the literature of wisdom, and thus raise the problem again whether we can speak of parallels or equations and whether Wisdom is equal to Logos or, on the contrary, they are two distinct principles. Let us see then the corresponding passages. Some of the quotations appeared above when we were looking for parallels of Pauline and wisdom texts. If we treat the parallels according to the principle of duality-unity instead of treating them as equations, and if we consider *arche* as a primal principle (that is as Sophia) and not only as a temporal category (as a beginning), and if we project the themes of the Old Testament and the New Testament onto each other (columns 1 and 2), a sophianic interpretation of John's Prologue will unfold (column 3).

Proverbs 8:22: The Lord possessed me in the beginning of his way [as arche, the beginning and primal principle of all else], before his works of old.	John 1:1a: In the beginning was the Word.	John 1:1a: *En arche* [Logos hidden in Sophia].

9. Schipflinger, *Sophia*, 65.

Genesis 1:1: In the beginning [arche, i.e., Sophia as primal image] God created the heaven and the earth.

Proverbs 8:30: I was by his side and set things in order.	John 1:1b: And the Word [Logos] was beside him.	John 1:1b: Logos/and Sophia/are companions of the Father.
Wisdom 8:3: [Wisdom] is the company of God.	John 1:2: [Logos] was in the beginning with God.	John 1:2: [Logos and arche, i.e., Sophia is with the Father since eternity.]
Wisdom 9:1: You created everything by your word and man by your wisdom.	John 1:3: All things were made by him; and without him was not any thing made that was made.	John 1:3: [The Father created all things with Logos and Sophia.]
Proverbs 8:35: For who finds me finds life, and shall obtain favour of the Lord. Wisdom 7:26: [Wisdom] emanates eternal light.	John 1:4: In him was life; and the life was the light of men.	John 1:4: [Sophia is the mother of life. Sophia and Logos bring supernatural life to all.]
Proverbs 1:24: I have called and you refused, I have stretched out my hand and no man regarded.	John 1:5: The light shines in darkness; and the darkness comprehended it not.	John 1:5: [Here begins the *kenosis* of Logos and Sophia.]

Proverbs 1:24: I have called, and ye refused; I have stretched out my hand, and no man regarded.	John 1:11: He came onto his own and his own received him not.	John 1:11: [Logos and Sophia go on Calvary together.]
	John 1:14: The Word was made flesh and dwelt among us.	John 1:14: [Christ is Logos embodied; Mary, i.e., the Church, Sophia embodied.]
	John 1:17: The law was given by Moses, but grace and truth came by Jesus Christ.	John 1:17: [The New Testament is the realization of the Old and it furthers the Torah, i.e., Wisdom.]

On the basis of this overview, the concept of Sophia can be seen in context. As we have noted, the Jewish and the minimalist Christian interpretations employ the theorem of a created Sophia in the theology of wisdom; however, this approach may take several forms. Which face has thus the many-faced (*polypoikilos*) Sophia (Ephesians 3:10)?

1. *The Cosmic Sophia*

The Lord possessed me as the arche of creation (viz. Prov 8:22) means that God created wisdom in primeval times as a primal principle or a model cause (*causa exemplaris*) or *entelechia* of all his subsequent creatures. On this level the mother of creation and the heart and soul of the world are all Sophia *archegetis*, the person-like beginning of the universe, its primary matter and image.

Sophia who dressed in the world as in clothing is the co-creator World-Soul, a cosmic principle of femininity.

Sophia who directs, organizes, and "informs" the creation of the world is Sophia *Eunomos* and Sophia *Harmosousa* (viz. LXX) or Sophia *Torah*: the order and harmony of the world.

This cosmic Sophia, then, is created and, even though the first of all creatures, is therefore not eternal, and thus is not on a level with the Son-Logos, who is God (viz. John 1:1).

2. *Sophia of Salvation*

Sophia who creates a people for herself by creating Israel is the mother of Sion and Jerusalem and their personification.

3. *Sophia Embodied*: *The Virgin Mary*

Sophia who became human in Mary, Sophia-Mary, is *Sophia incarnata*. By the overshadowing of Almighty God (Luke 1:35) Sophia-Mary is promoted to the status of mother of God or *Theotokos*.

4. *Sophia as Christ's Human Nature*

The Council of Chalcedon reached a synthesis according to which Christ's Divine and human nature are distinct and inseparable. Sophianic tradition holds that the human nature of Christ is Sophia (*humanitas Christi, natura humana Christi*). The Council of Ephesus refuted the former belief that Mary had given birth to Christ only as human, though, inevitably, had given birth to him in human form.

Some people see a parallel of the two natures of Christ in the Jungian concept of *animus-anima*. They speak of the androgyny of the Logos or a union of features of the two genders where *anima* is Christ's human nature, that is, Sophia, while *animus* is the *pleroma*, that is, his divine nature. It is in this figuratively dual gender that they see the reason why the Fathers equated Logos and Sophia. This idea seems to be confirmed by some mystics and visionaries such as Heinrich Suso, who discovered feminine features in churches and icons devoted to Sophia.

5. *Sophia as Christ's Mystical Body*

In Pauline teaching the Church, the bride and mystical body of Christ, can be seen as Christ's mystical body born by Mary (that is, Sophia embodied), and thus as an expansion of the Sophia-Mary dimension. Sophia is the bride of Logos, and as such co-operates with him in the work of redemption. Here again, she can be seen as embodied in the Church.

The Logos-Sophia connection as a sacred nuptial is confirmed by the fact that, according to Paul, Christ is the second Adam (1 Cor 15:42), to which conventionally the parallel figure of Eve, that is, Mary is added.

6. *The Apocalyptic Sophia*

The apocalyptic and eschatological Sophia means that mankind with the whole of the created world is going to reach an ultimate union with God (viz. "God will be all in all") and in this process of divine "rebirth" with God (viz. Rom 8:22), Sophia, like a mother, is going to take a part.

7. *Sophia and the Holy Trinity*

The elements of our image of Sophia each place Sophia on the level of created being. This practice results in an astounding conclusion: one cannot equate Logos with a created Sophia since Logos is a part of the divine nature; he is an eternally divine person (viz. God was the Word [Logos]). But then the question remains concerning how a cosmic Sophia is related to the persons of the Holy Trinity?

She is related to the Father as a Maiden created and accepted by the Father, the daughter of the Father, and, therefore, the sister of the Son.

We have already seen several aspects of Sophia's relation to Logos. However, from another perspective, Sophia is created by and presented to the Logos: she is his bride (*Costa Verbi*). This created Sophia is the gift of the Father to his Son. The essence of the being of Sophia, her turning toward the Logos, is nothing else than a response to the Word, a blessing uttered to the Logos.

Her relationship to the Holy Spirit can be described as an image created and adored by the Holy Spirit, or, according to Schipflinger, the reflection of the feminine and motherly principle within the Holy Trinity. We are going to address this hypothesis in the next chapter on the concept of the non-created Sophia.

The Maternal Face of God?

An Attempt to Validate the
Sameness of (Created) Sophia and Mary

In order to persuade the reader to accept that Mary is Sophia embodied, one should find textual proofs: who advocates or teaches this possibility? We have already seen testimonies from the Gospels. This teaching is realized in the history of God's people in the new covenant, in the faith of the centuries, and especially in the Marian devotion of the Eastern (Russian) Rite, but many wise authors have recognized this treasure in the West as well.

Furthermore, if we take this connection for granted, how can we express it in terms of theology and how does it relate to that other mystery, the hypostatic union of Logos? According to Schipflinger, the two mysteries are fundamentally different. While Logos embraces two distinct natures, those of the divine and the human, Sophia and Mary share a created nature, Sophia being purely spiritual (aeonian) and Mary her embodied earthly form. Schipflinger specifies in his theory that Mary consists of body and soul like any human being, yet her soul is Sophia, which is why the term *Sedes Sapientiae* is descriptive of her nature. The embodiment or incarnation of Sophia means that she becomes tangible in the human form of Mary.[10]

But from this point on Mary is no different from any other woman of contemporary Nazareth: an Israelite mother. The person of Sophia remains the same as before her embodiment in Mary, but the immanent essence of her person (from a phenomenological perspective) is now revealed in a different form: different from her aeonian existence, which had been her feature before and during creation. This human mode of Sophia's being can be likened to the experience of the Logos in Christ: while he bears the burdens of time and space, his original spirituality retreats and is hidden.

Although the hypostatic union of the Logos is not an accurate model of the union of Sophia and Mary—what He experiences is validated by Jesus: He reduced himself to human life (viz. Phil 2:7–

---

10. Schipflinger, *Sophia*, 328.

8). As we have seen, Wisdom goes through a similar experience (Prov 1:20). The above conditions apply to the being of Mary as well: Sophia can only reveal herself in her in a hidden mode.

The embodiment of Sophia compares to the manner in which the soul of man is bounded by his bodily form: the laws of matter curtail human souls. Our soul co-exists with our body that is weak and ill, asleep and restricted in self-expression. Likewise, Sophia lived a real human life in Mary: she took in food when hungry, learned, spoke, gave birth to a child, embraced him, cried, and felt the pain of mothers. Through the texture of her human existence, however, something of Sophia can be seen: her faith, her virtues, her wisdom, her purity, and her beauty. This is why the Holy Mother has become the muse of art and feminine ideals over the centuries.

Mary's sophianic identity is revealed in her readiness to accept the impossible upon the word of the angelic herald: she becomes the Mother of God (Luke 1:38). Our servant is the maiden who appeared in the image of Wisdom and who is a faithful companion of God (Wisdom 8:1–18). The consciousness of Sophia, who "from generation to generation enters the souls of saints," is echoed in the Magnificat: "all generations shall call me blessed" (Luke 1:48).

Let us see a few more details in Mary's life that reveal Sophia's presence in her. A sophianic trait in Mary is, so to speak, how she has Jesus perform the first miracle at the wedding at Cana. She becomes the spiritual mother of us all, like Sophia: "Behold thy mother" (John 19:27). Sophia-Mary will become the mother of the Church when Mary gathers the orphaned apostles (Acts 1:14). Sophia-Mary receives the Holy Spirit on the first Pentecost when she spiritually becomes the Mother of the Church. Catholic dogmas concerning Mary are also sophianic: in her immaculate conception, her existence without sin, and her assumption into heaven.

Yes, in her assumption Mary shakes off the bonds of time and space, and her virtues, her serving charity and philanthropy, can now become unlimited. The assumption of her body and spirit can be seen as her transformation into the "woman clothed with the sun" (Rev 12:1) and as her return to the spiritual and aeonian mode of being of Sophia. Her role as mediator emphasized by the Catholic and the Orthodox churches and her dignitary status as the Queen of

Heaven complete Mary's being in the mode of being of the created Sophia.

Most Catholics and Orthodox regard the Virgin Mary as their patron and queen. With her heavenly work she personifies femininity, motherhood, and eternal beauty. What had been expressed in the literature of wisdom or in the myths of other cultures in scattered form became complete in our heavenly Mary. She rejects everything that debases us: sin, hatred, evil, death.

So far we have made an ascent: starting from the earthly Mary we have reached the Queen of Heaven. However, the route in the opposite direction is also worth taking: let us investigate whether the features that we attributed to Mary, such as being free of all sin, including original sin, hold valid for Sophia as well, who is regarded as the Soul of the World. According to Schipflinger, original sin effected human (earthly) nature only, and thus the concept cannot be raised in relation to a cosmic Sophia.[11] Mary was not exempted from original sin "automatically" and would not have been exempt without Christ's redemption (viz. *redemptio "ante"*) but on account of the embodiment and redemption of Christ. The Ave Maria includes both elements: being totally free of sin and that it is so on account of Christ's embodiment. "Hail, thou that are highly favored, [...] thou shalt conceive in thy womb, and bring forth a son, [...] that holy thing which shall be born of thee shall be called the Son of God" (Luke 1:28, 31, 35).

As for being free of personal sin, this exemption is not conferred on Mary originally either, but she earns it by her human freedom and with her motherly service to the embodied Logos. Similarly, Sophia had free will. Absurdly, she could have turned away from God as Lucifer and the devils did. She was the totality of benevolence and beauty ("No uncleanliness infiltrates her," Wisdom 7:25) because she aligned herself to the will of the Father with her created freedom; just as in her embodiment Mary aligned herself to the will of God: "be it unto me according to thy word" (Luke 1:38).

As we have seen above, almost every icon representing the Annunciation depicts the unity of Sophia and Mary by showing the

11. Ibid.

figure holding a book in her hand or on her lap. Especially expressive are the Sophia icons. Also astonishing are the supplications of the Litany of Loreto, which can be interpreted properly in sophianic terms. Schipflinger sums up his thesis in his book on Sophia-Mary: "As the name of the embodied Logos is Jesus Christ, so is Sophia-Mary the name of the human Sophia. The totality of Sophia prophetically forecast in the Bible is attained in Mary and in the Church. This aspect clarifies which role Mary plays in Christ's salvation. Mary is not only a motherly but also a feminine companion of Christ; she co-operates with him, and had been a mediator in the creation and maintenance of the world and in the redemption and accomplishment of Israel."[12]

This new perspective allows us to fully understand *hyperdulia* or the veneration offered to Mary as she is ranked above all angels and saints (viz. the expressions of Greek liturgy: "most holy, most pure and most blessed" or "she who is esteemed higher than the cherubim"). Accordingly, we can view Mary from three aspects now:

1. As a simple, saintly woman, mother, and housewife.

2. As our patron and queen who is the mother of individuals and the Church as well, and who is the mother of mercy, healer of the sick, and helper of man.

3. As cosmic queen of heaven and earth, as World-Soul, and as mother of all peoples and as the justified bearer of the title of the Litany of Loreto.[13]

Furthermore, these three forms reveal the peculiar dimensions of the Virgin Mary, the Mother of God:

1. First, the natural-human dimension in light of which Protestants see her.

2. Second, the supernatural-heavenly or hyperdulic dimension in light of which the Catholic and Orthodox churches honor her.

3. Third, the cosmic, sophianic dimension in light of which especially the Russian Rite of the Eastern Church venerates her.

12. Ibid.
13. The same ornamental titles are present in the East in the Akathist Hymn.

On these propositions may be built a hypothetical fourth dimension, which is followed by a growing number of representatives of science, theology, psychology, and symbology.

The above are merely ideas to help us better understand the mystery of Sophia-Mary. It is up to theologians to investigate whether these mere ideas are worth formulating into a rigid doctrine similar to the mystery of the embodiment of the Logos.

This investigation has just commenced. Yet certain principles are already taking shape: the investigation, among others, must involve scientists, philosophers, and historians. Today, in an age of ecological crisis, the connection between Sophia and the cosmos ought to be clarified. The parallel of body and soul should also be addressed: Sophia is the soul of the world. This aspect may open grounds for representatives of natural sciences to step beyond the horizon of mere facts.

15

The Holy Spirit:
The Uncreated Sophia?

I N OUR ESSAY we have started out from the proposition that there are polarities at every level of being. This proposition is closely related to the Sophia-principle, according to which the highest polarity in creation is the unity of the Logos and Sophia. We have seen different representations of this in the field of philosophy, religion, and Christian revelation. However, the most important questions are the following: What are the divine roots of this polar structure? Is it possible for God to be present in being, and, if yes, in what form? And how can the feminine principle of being be present in the Holy Trinity?

As we have already seen at the end of Chapter 1, Christianity has an answer to the polar structure of being. It is the Holy Trinity, the principle of "one essence in three persons," and a form of faith that starts out from the duality of the Father and the Son and holds that the Holy Spirit is the unity of the two. According to Western trinitology, the Holy Spirit originates from those two persons (*abutroque*). In this system of thought none of the persons has a gender. The words "Father" and "Son" (*Pater, Filius*) are masculine. The expression Holy Spirit (*Spiritus Sanctus*) is also masculine in Latin, but in Greek it is neutral (*to Pneuma to Hagion*). The Holy Spirit is masculine in other languages as well: der *Heilige Geist* in German and *Spirito Santo* Italian. In Semitic languages, as we will see, the Holy Spirit is feminine (*Ruah*).[1] Both East and West believe that

---

1. The word *Ruah* (similarly to Hokmah) is also part of the Islamic vocabulary

man becomes the image of God (Gen 1:27) by experiencing the principle of "one nature in several persons," which may be extended to all aspects of existence.[2]

We have also seen that according to the so-called psychological theory of the Holy Trinity, the Son is born out of the "recognition" of the Father, and the Holy Spirit is born out of the "will" of the two. Here it is the Son, the Logos, who is regarded as Divine Wisdom, while the Holy Spirit is the representation of the will or love.

The idea according to which it is the Holy Spirit who might be the source of the Sophia-principle, its carrier in divine being and the female actor in the Holy Trinity, rarely surfaces throughout the centuries. (Although we are already familiar with the name of Theophilos of Antioch and we have seen such identification in various works of art.) Such intertwining of Sophia and the Holy Spirit and the feminine aspect of God might be surprising, even though it is not just a pious intuition. We will see that it has its roots in revelation. It is by no means more abstract or less real than the usual arguments presented by dogmatics concerning divine concepts such as the begotten, the breathed, the beloved, and so forth. All these arguments are valid to a certain extent, but the Gospel is considerably more specific when it talks about the Father, the Son, and someone else whom we may regard as a Mother.

Naturally there are objections to such an idea. The latest works in the field of dogmatics hold that "it is a theological mistake to draw a parallel between the masculine Logos and the feminine *Ruah* or Sophia embodied by Mary. . . . Mary is not hypostatically related to the third person of the Holy Trinity. She is not predestined to give a human form to the Soul of God."[3]

Many have tried to refute this "feminist" approach by saying that in scripture God does not have a gender. However, even traditionalists admit that God loves His people and the world both as a father

---

as *Ruh* along with *Ruhu'lqudus*, the Holy Spirit who reveals herself to the prophets and the saints ("spoke by the prophets" in the Christian Credo).

2. Ludwig Oeing-Hanhoff, "Trinitarische Ontologie und Metaphysik der Person," in *Trinität* (Freiburg: Herder, 1984), 143.

3. *Dogmatics* II. 188.

and a mother.[4] The Jungian approach might help us to recognize that both the feminine and the masculine are present in all of us, only in different proportions. It must be that way with God as well. We should admit that we have forgotten about the maternal side of God.

Just a few strokes of the brush about this forgotten face. We usually ignore the fact that in the Old Testament the name of God is not only the word El, which is probably masculine, or the word Elohim, which is usually interpreted as a plural form of that. God is also called Eloah, which is feminine and very likely the remnant of an earlier form of "goddess." We should also consider that Yahweh, the most important name of God, derives from the word *hava* (to be) just like the word Eve. And, according to Erich Fromm, the word *Sein* (being) is a feminine attribute.

But there are a number of other images as well. Numbers 11:12 compares the care of God to the image of a nurse: "Take care of them like a nurse takes care of a baby." According to Isaiah, the Lord cannot forget about His people just like a mother cannot forget about her baby: "Can a woman forget her sucking child, that she should not have compassion on the son of her womb?" (Isaiah 49:15). But His protecting and consoling role is that of the mother: "As one whom his mother comforts, so will I comfort you" (Isaiah 66:13).

The question is whether it is possible to go beyond metaphors and similes when we talk about the feminine side of God. Or, to put it differently: is the patriarchal, masculine approach that dominated the Christian interpretation of religion for two thousand years not a product of the male-centered social approach of the Ancient World and the Middle Ages?

Before rejecting the possibility of a new approach, we should have a closer look at what scripture teaches about this matter. The existence of the Holy Trinity is accepted by every Christian today: there is a Father, there is a Son, and there is a Holy Spirit. But how does the feminine element come into play? That is our most important question. It is Schipflinger who wrote the most openly about it.

4. *Dogmatics* I. 566.

He is the one who described the figure of Sophia-Mary the most effectively as well.[5]

The Spirit of Wisdom

The most important element is the word Spirit (*Ruah*) itself. *Ruah*, like the Greek *pneuma* and the Latin *spiritus* originates from the movement of the air, wind, and breath. Its etymology suggests "strong winds," and its primary meaning denotes "wind" or "breath." Anthropologically, it means "vitality," "will," "spiritual capacity," and "ego"; while theologically it means "the power of God," "the willpower of God," "prophetic force," and "creative vitality" (Gen 1:2) which acts as and is the spirit of God. The word Holy Spirit (*ruah hallodes* to *pneuma* to *hagion*) appears at several places in the Old Testament (Psalm 51:13 and Isaiah 63:10). According to the Book of Exodus, during the exodus *Ruah Yahweh*, the Spirit of God, played a decisive role.

We can draw a parallel between *Ruah Yahweh* and the Word of God (*davar, Logos*) in Genesis 1:2 and in other places as well. Here the parallel is the fact that the Word of God also creates; it is a principle that brings order to chaos. Other parallels: "By the word of the Lord were the heavens made; and all the host of them by the breath of his mouth" (Psalm 33:6). In Sirach 24 and Wisdom 7:22 the word, the spirit and even wisdom appear as interchangeable and sometimes interrelated.[6] All this implies the existence of some sort of polarity in the divine sphere, which is complemented by the duality of the Word and the Holy Spirit in the New Testament.

But the most decisive factor is that the word *Ruah* is feminine, similar to the case of the Hokmah. In Semitic languages, the gender of a word usually becomes apparent only from the context. However, the word *Ruah* is only about half a dozen times masculine and about seventy times *feminine* in the Old Testament,[7] which gives a

5. Schipflinger, *Sophia*, 319.
6. The Koran also clearly reflects the inner relationship between the Word and the Spirit of God: "I have taught you Writing and Wisdom, the Tora and the Gospel" (Koran 5:111). The internal bonds between the Soul and Wisdom are apparent.
7. *Dogmatics* I. 484.

new meaning to the second verse of the Bible: "And the Spirit of God (*Ruah Yahweh*) moved upon the face of the waters." The comparison conjures the image of the mother-bird brooding over her eggs.

Similar images may be found in a number of other religions as well. They are a reference to the Absolute, the Origin of Creation, who is a mother bird. The *Tao Te Ching* pictures the Tao as a bird protecting and feeding her chicks. Therefore, the approach according to which *Ruah Yahweh*, the Spirit of God, is feminine has considerable validity. As Franz Raurell argues, "God, as *Ruah*, appears primarily in the role of a mother: as a creator, sustainer and protector. [...] The God of the Bible is a God who is always in contact with life, which she created as a mother."[8]

In light of the above we should reconsider the interpretation of the creation of the first couple (Gen 1:16–27): "Let us make man in our own likeness. [...] So God created man in his own image, in the image of God created he him; male and female created he them." It is obvious that man and woman become the image of God together, which means that there are male as well as female characteristics present in God. The latter is *Ruah*, the Spirit. Moreover, God uses the plural when He says: "Let us create [...]." This is often regarded as the royal plural, or *pluralis maiesteticus*. However, if we consider that according to the wisdom literature, Wisdom is a co-creator (Wisdom 8:30 and 8:4) and feminine in gender, it becomes apparent that the basic pattern is already present at the very beginning.

The role of the Holy Spirit in creation also appears in the Psalm of Genesis: "You take away their [the creatures'] breath, they die, and return to their dust. You send forth your spirit, they are created: and you renew the face of the earth" (Psalm 104:29–30). Here there is no word regarding whether the Holy Spirit is masculine or feminine, but its nourishing role is easily recognizable. The rejuvenating character in the New Testament is an *epiton ornans* of the Holy Spirit, which is always present in Eastern liturgy.

The existence of an interrelationship between the Holy Spirit and Sophia can easily be shown. According to Wisdom 7:22, Wisdom

8. Franz Raurell, *Der Mythos vom männlichen Gott* (Freiburg: Olten, 1989), 58.

possesses "a spirit inside of her: she is intelligent, holy, unique, versatile and refined." The two concepts appear at a number of places: the spirit of Wisdom (Wisdom 7:7–14), "The breath of the strength of Wisdom [*Ruah*]" (Wisdom 7:25). According to Wisdom 1:6, Wisdom is a spirit who loves man. Schroer holds that the identity of *Ruah* and Sophia was created as a result of God sending His spirit to the prophets and, through the prophets, Wisdom (= the Spirit) reached the people.[9]

The literature of wisdom assumes that Sophia is a divine person: the entire reasoning of Wisdom 9:9–18 is based on the idea that no mortal can know God; we can only get to know Him through Wisdom. Therefore, Sophia is part of divine life. However, this is something inconceivable within the framework of the Old Testament. And this is the very place where the identity of Sophia and the Holy Spirit is pronounced: "who can know your counsel, unless you give Wisdom and send your holy spirit from on high?" (Wisdom 9:17).

There are further reasons to accept this identity: according to Isaiah 11:2 the son of David (the Messiah) will possess wisdom, but he will receive it from the Spirit of Yahweh. God will work through him by His spirit (Wisdom 7:11). Receiving him is the same as receiving the Spirit. Sophia is the giver of everything that is good (Prov 8:21; Wisdom 7:11); in the same way the Holy Spirit is "the fountainhead of all that is good and the giver of life" in the Byzantine liturgy. Furthermore, Wisdom is a gift of God (Wisdom 8:21) in the same way as the Spirit is. [...] This is echoed in the New Testament: wisdom can only be conveyed by the Spirit of God to people whose hearts are willing to learn (1 Cor 2:10–16 and 12:8; Eph 1:17). The believers teach each other "a language which is thought by the spirit" (1 Cor 2:13).

We apply to the Holy Spirit what the literature of wisdom says

9. Samuel Schroer, "Der Geist, die Weisheit und die Taube. Feministisch-kritische Exegese eines neutestamentlichen Symbols auf dem Hintergrund seiner altorientalischen und hellenistisch-frühjüdischen Tradition," in: *FZPhTh* 33 (1986): 225. Geist, 216.

The Holy Spirit: The Uncreated Sophia?

concerning Sophia based on this intimate relationship, unity, and identity. The final result is that we discover that the Holy Spirit is the "Spirit of Wisdom" (Deut 31:9). This approach has a number of followers in various traditions, even if most Fathers of the Church identify Sophia with the Logos. We have seen, however, that Sophia appears in every act of salvation as the partner, mother, or bride of the Son, the Logos. Therefore, identifying Sophia with the Logos would lead us astray. We might arrive at a solution, however, if we propose that Sophia constitutes a polar unity with the Logos in the act of creation. It would all make sense because the Logos (= *nous*) and Sophia (= *pneuma* = *psyche*) stand side by side even in Greek philosophy. Consequently, we have an immensely rich source of facts at our disposal based on the Old Testament alone.

The Spirit of Rebirth

Does the New Testament say anything about the identity of the Holy Spirit and Sophia and the female actor within divine being? Before answering this question, let us consider that in a spiritual sense the Gospel also assumes a masculine character in God when it calls Christ the only Son of God. In the original Greek text Christ is called *Monogenes Theos*, the only begotten Son of God (John 1:18). I hope it is not blasphemy to say that if we can talk about begetting and there is a father, then there should be a mother as well. Needless to say: begetting here has nothing to do with sexuality in a physiological sense. It is an analogy, an expression of the sexual role in a psychological or ontological sense. The Father is the active conveyor of divine life and the Son is the fruit.

This conclusion seems to be contradicted by the words of the Lord Jesus Christ, according to which in heaven people "neither marry, nor are given in marriage" (Luke 20:35). This, however, refers to those who have been saved, since in that sphere of being there is no physical existence. There is no paradise populated by beautiful *houris* like the one assumed by Muslims or the kind of sexual life believed to be taking place in the afterlife by Mormons and Moonies. However, a number of Christian theologians believe that the masculine and feminine characteristics are present in heaven as well in the form of a "spiritual Eros."[10] This condition must be a reflection of the masculine and feminine characteristics of divine being.

But in what way is the maternal side, the reception and radiation of divine life, present in divine existence?

It seems that there is specific data concerning the maternal side of divine being. It is related to the person of the Holy Spirit. The New Testament does talk about the feminine aspects of the Holy Spirit, which may be considered a revelation of the Holy Trinity from a theological point of view. The first place where there is mention of the Holy Spirit is the report concerning the baptism of Jesus by the Synoptics (Matt 3:13–17; Mark 1:9–11; Luke 3:21–22), but John also refers to it (John 1:32–34). The usual translation, according to which the Spirit descends in the form of a dove, can easily be misunderstood. Perhaps we should say: it "hovered like a dove" or "descended like a mother bird descends on her nest." The Greek word *peristera* or the Latin *columba* are both feminine and mean "golden dove." Therefore, it does not mean that the Holy Spirit became a dove similarly to the way the Logos became man. Rather, we are holding a symbol in our hands.

The symbol of the (mother) dove was well known to the Jews and it was used to symbolize the bride and bridal love (Wisdom 4:10; 5:2; 6:8): "Rise up, my love, my fair one, and come away" (Song of Songs 2:10). Even the most modern edition of the *Handbook of Dogmatics* acknowledges that there must be a wisdom-theological approach behind the concept of baptism,[11] which makes its sophiological dimension obvious.

If we take a look around, we will find this symbol in the religion of the neighboring peoples of the Jews as well. In Greek tradition the Peristera is the bird of Ishtar, the goddess of love. John the Evangelist was not afraid of adopting this concept. He also borrowed the concept of the Logos from the Greeks and Phylon, but he gave it a new meaning. We might say that it is the Holy Spirit who takes all the risks because She wants to express that She is nothing else but

10. Joseph Baltensweiter, *Die Ehe im Neuen Testament* (Zürich-Stuttgart: Neue Stadt, 1971), 94.
11. *Dogmatics* I, 504.

the framework of the love of God, the manifestation of the feminine inside of God, the divine Mother and Bride. The dove, then, symbolizes all that other religions experience in the form of goddesses, but their only authentic subject is the Holy Spirit.[12]

The words of the Father seem to contain the words of the Spirit-Mother: "You are my only beloved Son, in whom I find delight." The bird hovering above the child refers to Genesis 1:2. Therefore, what takes place is a new creation, the creation of the Pauline "divine man," in which process the Holy Spirit has as active role just as in the first creation.

However, there are some serious problems with regard to scripture. In St. Matthew, the angel tells Joseph twice about Mary that "that which is conceived in her is of the Holy Spirit" (Matt 1:18, 20). This is what stands in the Apostles' Creed as well: "Conceived of the Holy Spirit." It may seem that the above demonstrates the masculine role of the Holy Spirit. At the same time Christian tradition rejected the approach according to which the Immaculate Conception is theogony and Christ was begotten by the Holy Spirit. Even today, official dogmatics holds that in the interpretation of the idea of the Immaculate Conception "due to the transcendent nature of God we should avoid an approach which would imply that God begot Christ in a physical sense."[13]

The contradiction can be resolved with the greeting of the angel: "The Holy Spirit will come upon you and the power of the Highest will overshadow you; therefore also that holy thing which will be born of you will be called the Son of God" (Luke 1:35). Here the Holy Spirit possesses the above analyzed features: she descends like a mother bird, just as later happens at the Baptism of the Lord. The Highest One, the Father himself, is the one from whom the child comes: that is why he becomes the Son of God. The Holy Spirit only takes part as a co-creator, a Spirit-Mother, contributing to the Son's becoming flesh. This shows that what takes place here is not begetting but a new creation where the Holy Spirit, the Spirit of God descends just as at the first creation. The two acts: "the power of the

12. Schipflinger, *Sophia*, 319.
13. *Dogmatics* II, 189.

Highest" (the initiating role of the Father) and the "descent of the Holy Spirit" are not necessarily identical. Rather, they complement each other as a hierogamic unity. It is for such reasons that Schipflinger holds it would be better to change the wording of the Creed (conceived from the Holy Spirit) to "conceived by the Holy Spirit" and interpret it the following way: the Holy Spirit prepared Mary to receive and bear the Son of God and presented Mary with her own divine femininity.[14]

There are analogies to that also in the Oriental tradition. As Gregory Nazianzen wrote, the Logos "became a man, save for sin: for He has been conceived from a virgin, after she had been prepurified (προκαθαρείσης) with respect to soul and body through the Holy Spirit." [15] This purification was perhaps the preparation of Mary for maternity, by that she became a temple of the Logos. Similarly, John Damascene writes that, "After the *fiat* of the holy Virgin, the Holy Spirit came upon her according to the word of the Lord, which the angel spake. [The same Spirit] was purifying (καθαῖρον) her and furnishing for her a receptive potency of the Word's divinity."[16]

But the original wording can also mean that the Father placed his Son in the hands of *Ruah* (the divine Mother) and Mary took him from her by conceiving a son. The wording is also correct in the sense of co-creation: the incarnation is the fruit of the co-creation of the Father and the Holy Spirit, which therefore includes the work of the Holy Spirit. The words "The Holy Spirit will descend upon you" remind us of the concept of Shekinah: Mary is the sign of the presence of the Holy Spirit. She is Her (the Holy Spirit's) human manifestation in space and time. In Eastern liturgy Mary is referred to as the Ark of the Covenant, Church, and Garden of Eden.

The Gospel ascribes feminine properties to the Holy Spirit in several places. According to Luke, Jesus started his public activities by referring to the following in the Synagogue of Nazareth: he announced that he had been anointed by the Holy Spirit and he

---

14. Schipflinger, *Sophia*, 320.
15. Gregory Nazianzen, "Theophania," in *Oration* 38 (*PG* 36, 325B 41–42).
16. John Damascene, *Expositio fidei*, 46, II, 16–19.

was the completion of the work of the Spirit (Luke 4:18–21). The activities listed are all feminine in nature: to comfort, heal, save, etc. Later, when saying good-bye to his disciples, Jesus calls the Spirit a "Comforter" again and refers to it as one who teaches everything and reminds us all of what has been said (John 16:13). This Comforter is "the spirit of truth who will guide you into all truth" (John 16:13). These are the same characteristics that Wisdom 7:21 attributes to Sophia: "I have learned what is hidden and what is visible because [...] wisdom has taught me to do so." Teaching, reminding, patiently repeating—these are all activities practiced primarily by mothers with their children. They are maternal virtues and characteristics.

Chapter 3 of the Gospel According to John, in which Jesus speaks with Nicodemus, is particularly important in this regard, drawing a parallel between the secret of birth and rebirth: man is born into this world from the womb of a mother (3:4). It is obvious that to the new, divine life man is delivered by the Holy Spirit: "That which is born of the flesh is flesh; and that which is born of the Spirit is spirit" (3:6). This activity is definitely a feminine one. Verses 12 and 13 of John's Prologue bear a new meaning as well: bodily we are given life by our parents, but now that we have become the children of God: we are born not of blood, the instincts of the body or the will of man, but we are born of God. And within God we are born of the love of the Father and the Holy Spirit-Mother.

The symbolism of Whitsun also reflects the motherly role of the Holy Spirit. It cannot be an accident that Mary is present at the descent of the Holy Spirit (Acts 1:14) and the birth of the Church, in the same way as she was present at the conception of the Son of God. It suggests that Mary is the incarnation of divine Wisdom and therefore has a maternal role in the birth of the body of Christ as well as in the Spiritual birth of the Church by the Holy Spirit.

Sophianic literature usually stops here, even though we know that Acts is the Gospel of the Holy Spirit. The linguistic miracle of Whitsun reminds us of the radiation of wisdom that creates holy men and sages. Peter specifically refers to this relationship in his Whitsun speech: "I will pour out my spirit upon all flesh; and your sons and daughters will prophesy" (Acts 2:17). Again, what we see is the protecting and nurturing love of the mother at work. We have seen before that the spread of the Church is the progress of the life of the Sophia-Church. It is nothing else but another descent of the Holy Spirit. In the same way as the Spirit spoke by the prophets, now it speaks with the words of its apostles. That is why the apostles said at the first Council: "It seemed to the Holy Spirit and to us" (Acts 15:28).

We have already analyzed the Sophia-concept in St. Paul. Paul applies much from the theology of wisdom to the Logos, but these parallels can be interpreted within the framework of the Logos-Sophia/bride-bridegroom relationship as well. This duality and unity is a justified element of the gospel of Paul. But to what extent can the elements of Sophia be applied to the Holy Spirit in the work of Paul?

St. Paul links Wisdom and the Holy Spirit at a number of places. He views Wisdom as a gift of the Holy Spirit (Eph 1:17). He applies various elements of Hokmah-theology to the Holy Spirit: "The spirit searches all things, even the deep things of God" (1 Cor 2:10). Paul contrasts the bodily man and spiritual man at a number of places, thereby suggesting that we are born by the Spirit into this higher form of life (Rom 8:6–12) since She is the Soul by whom we can say to God: Father, we are brothers and coheirs of Christ (8:16–17), a complement to our earlier analysis concerning John 1:1 and 3:6 as well.

Paul paints a surprisingly motherly image of the Holy Spirit when he says "we are carrying the seeds of the Soul" (Rom 8:23). To that he relates the image according to which "every creature sighs and is laboring with us" (8:22) and the Spirit sighs with us (8:26). It is the same act as what we have seen concerning the Church-Sophia and the cosmic Sophia: the Holy Spirit and the Church are the soul of the universe and they promote the salvation and divinity of the Church and the entire created world with motherly love.

We can also see the image of the woman pregnant with salvation in Revelation 12:1–6 representing the story of incarnation and its realization. Regardless of whether "the woman dressed in sunshine" is the representation of Mary or the Church, it is another description of Mary-Sophia and Church-Sophia from an eschatological perspective. The Holy Spirit is not mentioned in Revelation, but the author refers to "What the Spirit says to the Church" (Rev 1:7, 11) in the entire work. Consequently, the woman in labor with salvation is the ultimate revelation of the Spirit.

The Spirit and the bride (Mary as well as the Church) appear next to each other on the last page of scripture as well (Rev 22:17). They shout together: come to us. This does not mean that Mary is the bride of the Holy Spirit as it says in the pious songs of the common people. Rather, we can see the maternal side emerge again in contrast with Christ, who represents the male principle. It is the Eternal Feminine, the manifestation of the God-Mother on earth. It is Mary-Sophia, the Church-Sophia, who wants to nourish and nurture and who wants to radiate life just like her original pattern on earth, the first Eve (*Hava* = Life, the mother of life), did. This is how the image of the Holy Spirit becomes complete in the revelation as a Divine Female Person.

The Afterlife of the Image of the Holy Spirit with a Maternal Face

In spite of clear references in scripture, the feminine side of the Holy Spirit has been forgotten in the past due to cultural and historical reasons. Everyday thinking was dominated by the influences of a patriarchal way of life, and the Church was no exception. There were, however, people who tended to rely on a biblical background. Of the early Christians, St. Cyprianus said that the blessed virgins were the "most beautiful images of the Holy Spirit." In the 4th century, Didaskalia called the deaconesses of the early Church "the image of the Holy Spirit." St. John Chrysostom calls the Holy Eucharist "the milk of the motherly breast of the Holy Spirit." We have already mentioned the names of Irenaeus and Theophylos of Antioch who also identified Sophia with the Holy Spirit.

The strongest voice of the early Christian tradition is represented by Syriac theology. Although Syriac theology and literature were early, before the era of the great synods, it is nevertheless important, since the Syriac language is Semitic, related to Aramaic (the language spoken by Jesus)—and the *Ruah* for the Syrians was also a feminine being.[17] This theology is so valuable precisely because it is ancient. Syriac spirituality wanted to remain independent from Greek and Byzantine influences. That must be one of the reasons why it managed to develop its own ideas concerning this matter. St. Ephraim the Syrian (†373), whom the classics call "the Harp of the Holy Spirit," describes with similes and images (primarily with the image of warmth and fire) his experiences concerning the efficacy of the Spirit: "For Truth radiates from the Father by the Son, which gives life to everything by the Holy Spirit.[18]

The Syriac custom, which depicts the origin of the Holy Spirit with female symbols,[19] seems to be an important phenomenon for Spirit-theology today. According to Syriac pneumatology, the Holy Spirit originates from the rib of the Logos, where the prefiguration is the creation of man. Similar to Eve, who was formed from the rib of Adam and is the mother of life, the Spirit is the rib of the Logos and the mother of new life. She unites those born of the life of God in the new community of the Church. Later in the West, the Church is born from the side of the Crucified (from the water-blood). However, all the above indicate that both the Church and the Holy Spirit are feminine and maternal concerning their nature.

We can draw the following parallels: Adam = Logos, Eve = Soul, the life of the sons of man = the life of the sons of God (in the Church). In contrast with Eve stand not only Mary and the Church but the Holy Spirit as well. Therefore, she also becomes more pneu-

---

17. This question has an immense literature. Among the most important are the following: G. Tüttő, *Femininity in the Holy Trinity and in our World* (Essex, UK: McCrimmon Publishing Company, 2004); K.E. McVey "Ephraem the Syrian's Use of Female Metaphors to Describe the Deity," *Journal of Ancient Christianity* 5 no. 2 (2001): 261–88; S. Brock, "The Holy Spirit as Feminine in Early Syriac Literature," in *After Eve: Women, Theology and the Christian Tradition*, ed. J.M. Soskice, 73–88 (London: Collins Publishers, 1990); R. Murray, *Symbols of Church and Kingdom: A Study in Early Syriac Tradition* (Cambridge: Cambridge University Press, 1975); Y. Congar "I Believe in the Holy Spirit," in *The Motherhood in God and the Femininity of the Holy Spirit* (London: Chapman, 1983), 155–64; S. Coakley, *Femininity and the Holy Spirit in Mirror to the Church: Reflexions on Sexism* (London: SPCK, 1988).

18. *Sermo* 80, 2.

19. Of course, her origin from the Father is without *Filioque*.

matologically complete in the Church: a fact that is recognized even by the rather traditional dogmatics of today.[20]

The Syrian fathers emphasize the omnipotence of the Spirit. In their writings the "dove" represents the bridal relationship of the Father and the Spirit and the maternal relationship of the soul and creation. Early Syrian witnesses call the soul a mother while attributing a second role to her in the Trinity, which presents a dogmatic problem to many. But if we take a closer look, we will see that there is a circular interrelationship (*perichoresis, circumincessio*) between the persons of the Holy Trinity without any kind of subordination, a condition which was strongly emphasized by the early Church.

According to Yves Congar, "It is in the linguistic and cultural domains of Judaism and the Syriac world that the Holy Spirit is most frequently called 'mother.'" In the climate of Judeo-Christianity, this occurred especially in the Gospel of the Hebrews or the Gospel of the Nazarenes, which are mentioned by Clement of Alexandria, Origen, and Jerome. In Jerome, we read of the coming of the Spirit on Jesus at the time of his baptism, with the words "You are my beloved Son." In the Odes of Solomon, which originated in Syria, the Dove-Spirit is compared to the mother of Christ who gives milk, like the breasts of God. In the Syrian liturgy, the Spirit is compared to a merciful mother, and Aphraates, a Syrian writing in Persia c. 336–345, wrote that "the man who does not marry respects God his father and the Holy Spirit his mother, and he has no other love."[21]

Besides the Syriac tradition, Armenian theology considers the Holy Spirit as mother, according to a comment by His Beatitude Gregoire Pierre XX Ghabroyan, Patriarch of Cilicia of the Armenians, head of the Synod of the Armenian Catholic Church, at the 2015 Family Synod. In fact, there are some Eastern Churches, the Maronite Catholic Church, for example, where the ancient Aramaic-Syriac language is used in liturgy and in which the Holy Spirit is feminine in gender.

Due to the teachings of Syriac theology, even the rather reserved official dogmatics of today acknowledge that "Although we should

---

20. *Dogmatics* I, 568.
21. Y. Congar, *I Believe in the Holy Spirit*, 157.

be very careful when based on writings concerning the history of salvation we conclude the immanence of the Trinity, it seems rather encouraging for pneumatology that in the Study of Creation, Mercy and the Church we call the Spirit the Mother of Creation, the Recreated Mother, and the Mother of the Church."[22] Then what could keep us from discovering the maternal face of God in the internal life of the Holy Spirit as well? This text is a description of the Spirit's activity in the Economy of Salvation. But—according to the doctrine of Karl Rahner—this dimension of the Trinity is always an expression of the "immanent" Trinity also.[23] Then we can research the maternity of the Holy Spirit.

Let us continue with the testimonies. In the Church of Urschalling in Bavaria there is a depiction of the Holy Spirit from the 9th century, the age of Prince Tasilo and Charles the Great, where the Holy Spirit is depicted as a woman between the Father and the Son.[24] The picture reveals that such thought was not uncommon in that age. The Coronation of Mary by Dietric Bouts also belongs to this category.[25] It can be considered a Catholic representation of Mary because Mary is brought into a direct relationship with all three persons of the Holy Trinity. She is the daughter of the Father, the mother of the Son and she is always represented in a vertical line under the Holy Spirit (just as in the case of Russian icons). Often they are represented in a common aureole, suggesting that they constitute one life-principle.

Scholasticism rejects the idea of the feminine, maternal nature of the Holy Spirit. It does so seemingly for philosophical and biological reasons that many people today would consider false. The real reason for doing so is a patriarchal way of thinking. St. Thomas Aquinas was the only one to raise the question of whether a female person should be regarded as the manifestation of the Holy Spirit. His question proves that he was an independently thinking philoso-

22. *Dogmatics* I, 542.
23. Ibid.
24. Appendix XVIII. The depiction of the Holy Spirit in the middle reveals a parallel with the Holy Trinity icon of Feofan Grek.
25. Appendix XIX.

182

pher. Unfortunately, he reached a negative conclusion. To him, woman is a passive being: she has a passive role both at conceiving and giving birth. She is nothing more than a biological net. Due to her passivity, woman cannot be the manifestation of the Holy Spirit for God is "*actus purus*" = pure act.[26] St. Thomas interprets wisdom as a virtue and the result of human effort: "*Sapientia est cognitio ex causis.*" Unfortunately, he failed to recognize the more profound message of the literature of wisdom.

At the beginning of the early modern age, even Meister Eckhart thought in similar Scholastic terms. His approach was that only man, the perfect being, can beget something perfect. The Perfect One can only beget a man. In the philosophy and theology of the Ancient World and the Middle Ages woman is an imperfect and unhappy creature.

Matthias Scheebennek, on the other hand, who lived about a hundred years ago, distinguished himself in Catholic theology by recognizing the feminine-maternal features of the Holy Spirit and by laying down the theological foundations of such an approach. Unfortunately, not many dared to follow him; the time was not yet ripe for the idea.

Today, however, due to a large extent to the spread of feminist theology, the question is becoming increasingly pressing: Are we right to regard God only from a patriarchal point of view? In other words: there is a Father and there is a Son. But where is the Mother? The answer is to be found in the Gospel: the Holy Spirit is the Mother. This revelation, however, fell under the censorship of patriarchal thinking. Women's demands for equal rights raise not only certain scientific and sociological questions, but theological ones as well. In light of that, we should reconsider our interpretation of scripture.

Many refuse to accept the idea of the "feminization" of the Spirit in the name of some sort of intellectualism. But abstract speculations will not take us much further, either. There has been progress in the interpretation of revealed truths, and that is exactly what progress in the field of dogmatics means. Why should we not wit-

26. *Summa c. Gentiles* IV, "De generatione Verbi."

ness or even play an active role in another connection where the Father-Mother-Son approach prevails?

It was the Lord Jesus Christ himself who said concerning the Holy Spirit's role in correcting the narrow-mindedness of his contemporaries and leading them to the recognition of the truth: "I have yet many things to say to you, but you cannot hear them now. [...] The Holy Spirit will guide you into all truth" (John 16:12). It took centuries for the followers of Christ to conceptualize the secret of Christ, the Holy Trinity, and Mary; and it took more than 1900 years to unveil the secret of the Immaculate Conception of the latter.

Perhaps we will soon reach a new stage of development concerning this question as well by applying a broader approach to the interpretation of the concept of the Holy Trinity and God instead of the one-sided, male-centered, patriarchal one. In this new approach, the Holy Spirit is the original source of femininity and Sophia-Mary is Her perfect reflection. She also manifests Herself in the Church, in every mother and every woman. That is what Pope John Paul I must have referred to when he referred to "God—our Father, but even more so—our Mother."

Does the above mean that Mary is the incarnation of the Holy Spirit in the same way as she is the incarnation of the cosmic Sophia or as Christ is the incarnation of the Logos? Our answer is: no. Schipflinger, the great sophiologist, would accept that Mary is the incarnation of the created, cosmic Sophia, but regarding her relationship with the Holy Spirit he only goes as far as saying that the revelation alludes to Mary being the image and icon of the Holy Spirit.[27]

It seems as if the revelation was to set a certain limit at this point. Although the greeting of the angel places Mary and the Holy Spirit next to each other, it regards them as separate persons. One of them is a divine person, the other one is a creature. The last lines of scripture also refer to the Spirit and the bride as separate persons (Rev 22:17) regardless of whether it means Mary or the Church. However, concerning efficacy in the practice of mercy and maternity, they stand on the same side.

27. Schipflinger, *Sophia*, 322.

The Holy Spirit: The Uncreated Sophia?

It is also hard to define the relationship between the Holy Spirit (even as non-created Sophia) and the created, cosmic Sophia. If Mary is the incarnation of the cosmic Sophia and a person different from the Holy Spirit, it is obvious that the same will also hold for the cosmic Sophia. She cannot be identified with the Holy Spirit: she is only the mirror of the Holy Spirit. She is the created continuation of the work of the Holy Spirit. In other words: she is the Shekinah of the Holy Spirit.

On the side of the Logos we can establish the following line: the only Son of the Father and the Logos of creation (John 1:3) are identical. The Logos was made flesh (John 1:14), and thus formed a hypostatic union with the human nature of Christ. However, we cannot do the same for the line of the Holy Spirit. Although as a Spirit-Mother the non-created Sophia (the Holy Spirit) may be the maternal partner of the Father, and the Son is born by the two of them (from all eternity), the cosmic Sophia is only her created image-icon, whose existence reminds us of the angels (and she is often depicted as such in iconography). She is the created colleague of the creator who became flesh in the Divine Parent. Therefore, we cannot say that the Holy Spirit formed a hypostatic union with Sophia or Mary. Sophia's incarnation is the Church, the bride and body of the Logos.

There are some who still reason along the line of Holy Spirit–World Spirit–Virgin Mary–Church on the analogy of the incarnation of the Logos. In that case, Mary would be the incarnated Holy Spirit and a divine person, an approach that has been rejected by most traditions. However high the East places the Divine Parent, it always insists on her being a created one. It is quite apparent, for example, in liturgy: Christ sacrifices himself for everyone but "especially for the Virgin Mary." Therefore, Mary is not a divine person.

The new sophianic pneumatology raises an additional question. The psychological interpretation of the Holy Spirit, which is the most widespread approach in the West and which is the product of the logosophic branch of Patristics, regards the Logos as the carrier of divine Intelligence and views the Holy Spirit as the manifestation of the will and love. Here in the new sophianic trinitology the Holy Spirit is the non-created Divine Wisdom. The two approaches can be reconciled if we consider the duality and unity of *anima and animus, ratio and intellectus, essentia and actus existendi.* The Holy Spirit is the unifying, maternal principle of Divine Intelligence, while the Logos is its actualizing, masculine side. The two make a perfect unity and form an efficient *hieros gamos* together similarly to how the Holy Spirit hovers above the waters of creation from the beginnings of time and at the same time everything is born in and by the Logos (John 1:3, 10). The two trinitologies look at two different sides of the same *perichoresis,* but the two together constitute a unity. Based on the *perichoresis, the circumincessio,* the different Holy Trinity models of the Church may be reconciled with each other.

And here we have to stop. Today there are different trinitologies. Not only Western and Eastern, but psychological, interpersonal, dialogical, the trinitologies of Karl Rahner, Pannenberg, Moltmann, and others. God is an incomprehensible mystery and the models are different "coordinate-systems," all of them taking only one aspect or another of the totality.

Is it possible to have a sophian trinitology?

We see that the traditional Western system is "set out from the Economy of Salvation,"[28] where the Holy Spirit comes "after" the work of the Father and Son, in as much as he "originates from the Father and the Son." For Eastern theology, the origin of the Spirit from the Father is an ontological expression, a description of the inner-trinitarian life. On the matter of the history of salvation, the East does not uses the *Filioque,* but accepts the expression: the Father operates "through the Son" ("*dia Hyiou*") and "in the Holy Spirit." Thus the two systems can be reconciled.

Can the maternity of the Holy Spirit be reconciled with these conceptions?

Certain Eastern theologies can without doubt be reconciled to associating the Holy Spirit with a sophianic maternity. As to Western interpretations, the maternal role of the Spirit in the Economy of

28. *Dogmatics* II, 559.

Salvation is perhaps easily acceptable, for he (she) is the principle of our rebirth.

But according to modern theology "the Trinity in the Economy of Salvation and the immanent Trinity are identical."[29] Then the maternity (as appropriation) is perhaps also present in the inner life of God. If the Holy Spirit is the non-created Sophia, (s)he is the partner of the Creator. If we accept that the *Arche* (of John 1:1) is the Holy Spirit, as the maternal principle of the Holy Trinity, then perhaps we can say that the Logos is present in her, "*in Arche*," as in a maternal womb in a kind of eternal "bearing." Thus the Logos is begotten from the Father, and bears the "Arche-Spirit" from eternity. The Spirit is the mother dove (*peristera*), who together with the Father declares Christ as the beloved Son. She is *vinculum caritatis*, identical with the love of God. The Psalms say: "You are my Son, I gave birth to you today."[30] Can this be also the confession of the Spirit?

In addition, tradition considers "generation" as the activity of the Father and the *primogenitus* of the Son. But bearing supposes the activity of the mother. Of course these words sound symbolic, but they are perhaps conducive to a new perspective. If we take this word (first-born) strictly (*protogenetos* = first begotten as result of the activity of man), it can also imply (or at the least does not exclude) the unity of the partner, the receptive side of the mother.

One last remark. Both West and East confess the monarchy of the Father. This principle is preserved also in a sophiological interpretation. Surely, the source of the Holy Spirit is also the Father, an analogy to the words of St. Paul: "As the man is the head of the woman and Christ is the head of the Church" (Ephesians 5:23), the Father is the origin of the Spirit-Mother. But let us view these systems on a wholly abstract level. The trinitology of the Eastern Church starts out from the monarchy of the Father, as from a *Monas* (= Father), from whom *Dyas* (= Logos and Holy Spirit) originates and the final result is *Trias* (Holy Trinity). This model describes the internal life

---

29. Ibid., 557.
30. Psalm 2:7, viz. "First-born of God," John 1:18.

(= *ousia*) of God. The usual Western model (after acknowledging the monarchy of the Father) focuses on the Father (= *oikonomia*) where the basis is the polarity of the Father and the Son. The unity of this polarity is the Holy Spirit (*abutroque*). The sophianic trinitology admits the Father's monarchy, but in a second step regards the relationship of the Father and the Holy Spirit-Mother as a starting point whose fruit is the Son. In creation, it regards the Logos and the World Soul-Sophia (the icon of the Holy Spirit) as a polarity from which the world is realized. These systems are equivalent, due to the circular interrelationship (*circumincessio*) between the Divine Persons.

With regard to the order of the Divine Persons, we have seen that there were witnesses (e.g., the early Syrian theologians) who attributed the second-place role to the Spirit in the Trinity, which presents a dogmatic problem to many. But there is a circular interrelationship (*perichoresis, circumincessio*) between the Persons of the Holy Trinity without any kind of subordination, which was strongly emphasized by the early Church. All three relations (Father-Son, Father-Spirit, and Son-Spirit) can be investigated both separately and together. Of course the monarchy of the Father is doubtless.

The trinitology based on perichoresis goes beyond the schizophrenia that has characterized Western thinking since Parmenides and Heraclitus. According to traditional Western thought, being and becoming are two separate things and the core of being is stationary and never-changing (*kinesis akineton, primus motor non movens*). However, the internal life of the Holy Trinity is not characterized by immobility. It is the interrelationship of the three persons. It is movement, not in a sense of transformation, but in a sense of turning toward each other, in a sense of self-sacrifice. It is *Sein* and *Werden* at the same time, which is why it can be the driving force of all change and development. In other words: it is the process of love, for God is love (1 John 4:16). We might even say: it is *Hieros Gamos,* or Holy Love. It is the turning toward each other of the Father and the Spirit, which gives place to the eternal birth of the Son who "was born before the beginning of time."

16

Conclusions: A New Theological Perspective

H OPEFULLY, the discovery of Sophia will result in a new perspective in theology. If we approach other religions in the
open spirit of the Second Vatican Council, we realize a
meta-theological, holistic, ecumenical strand and recognize that in
almost all great religions a feminine or motherly side of divine
being is present, either in the form of a divine person or in the form
of an immanent, organizing principle like the cosmic Sophia.

We had to realize that these two forms can be found in the Judeo-
Christian tradition. The manifestations of the Christian tradition,
including the teachings of Catholic, Orthodox, and Protestant faiths
alike, shed light on the fact that, based on scripture, a created
Sophia as World-Soul exists and we can see her embodiment in the
Church and in the Holy Virgin, Mother of God. We concluded that
in divine being it is especially the Holy Spirit who best represents
the feminine face of the divine, but by saying this we are not chal-
lenging the conventions of the Holy Trinity or pneumatology.
Divine life is so profoundly infinite that it accommodates newer
and newer approaches, as, for example, with the different inroads of
Eastern and Western trinitologies.

Here we have to make our point unmistakably clear: a credible
sophiology does not carry the notion of a new revelation and it does
not question established Christian doctrines. Any sophiology that
recognizes new figures beside and beyond the persons of the Holy
Trinity, like the adherents of Trinosophia, whose followers argue for
the parallel triad of the Mother, Daughter, and Holy Intellect, can
compromise our ability to appreciate the sources (the literature of

wisdom, and the writings of Eastern and Western sophiologists), which a credible sophiology also employs.[1]

Such theosophical and Anthroposophical approaches misunderstand the messages of revelation and tradition completely. As we have seen, Christian revelation does provide a basis on which to find the role of the maternal and the feminine in divine being without initiating a fourth person in the Holy Trinity. We only have to recognize that the Holy Spirit bears this feminine face; the Holy Spirit is the Spirit-Mother, if you like, and a distinct Mother-Sophia or Holy Soul is quite unnecessary once these features are present in the Holy Spirit.

And there is no need for a distinct Daughter-Sophia either, since the presence of the Holy Spirit encapsulates this feature as well: the World-Soul or the primeval *entelecheia* or the mother and heart of the world, which many followers regard as a person and who is the companion of the Father and, from another perspective, of Logos in the creation of the world. And the embodiment of this World-Soul-Sophia and perhaps the icon of the Holy Spirit is Sophia-Mary, mother of God, in whom Logos became man and whose further embodiment is the Church or the bride of Christ. Thus, there is no need for any new trinosophia, especially if it is blended with astrology and results in a kind of new Christianity, which sees the Lamb of God and the coming of the end of times by accepting such gnosis.

Any syncretistic attempt, such as Moonism and Mormonism, which, by seeking the motherly face of divine being, reaches the element of *hieros gamos* but leans toward polytheism, is ultimately the illegitimate dilution of Christian faith.

Yet we do need to discover the Sophia of Holy Scripture and Christian tradition, many of whose features other religions, philosophies, and sciences also recognize.

This discovery demands of us a new theological mentality as well. To take a geometrical example: a new system of coordinates does not discard those already present (the Eastern or Western trinitology in our case) but offers a new approach. Here our basis in divine

---

1. Robert Powell, *The Most Holy Trinosophia and the New Revelations of the Divine Feminine* (New York: Lindisfarne Press, 2000).

Conclusions: A New Theological Perspective

life is the hierogamic relationship of the Father and the Holy Spirit
(Spirit-Mother) and the fruits of this relationship are the Son (*ad
intra*) and the created world (*ad extra*).

Revelation does not tell us much of this aspect of divine life. It
only talks about begetting (viz. *protogennetos* = first begotten), but
by a simple inversion the concept alludes to delivery and the mother
as well. And if we accept the principle that the immanent Holy Trinity can be equated with the Trinity of salvation, that is, the latter
expresses the former, and we accept that, according to the new
sophianic perspective, the "Ave Maria" reflects the existential principle of the Holy Spirit, then we can describe divine life not only
through an eternal begetting but also through an eternal delivery
and, in fact, an eternal love and nuptial bond between the Father
and the Holy Spirit (Spirit-Mother). Of course, we are not talking
about carnal love or sexuality, but, rather, the gift of being, the gift
of life: the most sacred and highest personal giving[2] that is the primeval model of all created polarities, and the vital source of love,
marriage, and any relationship in the sphere of man.

In the light of this love-relationship we can see the detail frequently appearing in theological debates ("the Spirit of truth, which
proceeds from the Father" [John 15:26]) from a new angle. As the
woman "was taken out of man" (Gen 2:23), so that male and female
together reflect the image of God (Gen 1:27), likewise, their model,
the Father and his Spirit-Mother companion originating from the
Father together comprise a unified being; and the fruits of their life-
giving power are the Son and the entire world created in the Son,
for the Son, and by the Son (viz. John 1:3). When the Fathers of the
East were reluctant to accept the doctrine that the Holy Spirit originates from the Son as well as from the Father, they, perhaps, consciously or unconsciously brought to mind that the *Filioque* is an
expression of the Economy of Salvation (mission of the Spirit
"after" the work of the Father and the Logos-Son), while the Son's

2. The patristic principle (the Son is "eternally born of the Father without a
mother") only denies begetting in a carnal sense of the word and does not necessarily refute life-giving symbolically.

origin from the Father is in the East an inner-trinitarian process (viz. the verb *proerchomai*, John 15:26).

But let us return to the relationship of the Father and the Spirit-Mother. In the description of this highest *hieros gamos*, the notions of Eastern trinitology may prove helpful. As we have seen, the East is ready to accept the dichotomy of potential and act or *dynamis-energeia* in divine being because it recognizes the passive potential beside the active one. Could we describe the relationship of the Father and the Spirit-Mother with the dichotomy of potential and act?[3] The Spirit is the receptive side of divine being awaiting impregnation, the totality of motherhood in God's self-expression, and this is why it can float "over the waters" during creation and in the work of embodiment as well. The Father is indeed the Almighty Power who animates the seeds of being hidden in the Spirit. Logos, on the other hand, transforms the seeds of his life into the elements of the world.

The primary reflection of the sacred nuptials in divine being and, in a broader sense, of the Holy Family, is Creation. Therefore, the ultimate organizing power of creation is a hierogamic relation again: the love-relationship of Logos and the World-Soul (created Sophia). This nuptial-like relation is reflected on a small scale in all beings as the relation of matter and form, potential and act, the orders of substance and being, and as the duality and unity of body and soul in man, and further as the relationship of man and woman: marriage and family, on the level of interpersonal relations. The embodiment of Logos is Jesus Christ, of the World-Soul is the Mother of God, who then became the mother of the Church; therefore, both are sources and vehicles of divinity and work toward fulfilling the purposes of the world.

This new theological perspective which identifies the divine roots of femininity demands a wise attitude: we have to recognize that our one-sided, masculine, and patriarchal view of God is not credible and, for the same reason, our views of the Church and of man

---

3. The dichotomy of matter and spirit will not be sufficient here, but on the plane of created being such dualities are the reflections or projections of potential and action in the divine.

are also biased. The discovery of the maternal face of God would help us to attain the emancipation of the sexes, to recognize their unity and dignity through appropriate interpretation of marriage and sexuality, and to find woman's place in the Church and in everyday life as they deserve.

On the basis of Sophia, a new spirituality may be born that could pave the way for advocates of nature conservation and members of the Green movement, by encouraging them to foster a spiritual relationship with Sophia as World-Soul even in the form of a cult.[4] If we observe feasts of "all heavenly powers," of angels, in both the Eastern and the Western Church, why should we not celebrate Hokmah-Sophia or the World-Soul as well?[5] We could consciously undertake to use maternal features of the Holy Spirit in certain liturgical forms and this sophianic pneumatology might enrich charismatic and Pentecostal spiritual movements that are already flourishing.

4. A faithful depiction of this movement could be Appendix XX: Earth-Mother, painted at the end of the 20th century, in Romania.

5. Thomas Schipflinger lists a number of prayers addressed to Sophia-Mary in his book on sophiology (Sophia-Maria).

Epilogue

Femininity in the
Holy Trinity and in Our World

The Catechism of the Catholic Church (694–701) lists several biblical symbols of the Holy Spirit: water, fire, cloud and light, hand, finger, and, mainly, dove. The Holy Spirit is traditionally represented as a *dove* with outspread wings. In the Bible there are several passages about God with wings: wings are symbols of the protective and comforting love of God. None of the above symbols of the Holy Spirit, including the dove, indicates that the Holy Spirit is a person, a Divine Person.

I venture to suggest that the dove with outspread wings and with a woman's face, placed between the image of the Father and the image of the crucified Christ, may better convey our human understanding of the Holy Spirit and the function of the Spirit.

A female face may convey the femininity in God who is love (1 John 4:16). God the Father's love is revealed in creating us through the Holy Spirit (Giver of life) to the image of his only begotten Son. I am confident that the ideals of femininity are beautifully reflected in the function of the Holy Spirit, the Giver of life, the Paraclete (John 14:16 and 26), which can mean Advocate, Comforter, Intercessor, Protector, Support. The same ideals of femininity are also beautifully reflected in the gifts of the Holy Spirit: wisdom, understanding, counsel, strength, piety, knowledge, and fear of the Lord (viz. Isaiah 11:1–3) and in the fruits of the Holy Spirit: love, joy, peace, patience, goodness, gentleness, fidelity, humility, self-control, and purity of heart (viz. Gal 5:22–23). Besides the gifts and fruits of the Holy Spirit, which are given for the growth in holiness in the life of individual Christians, there are other gifts of the Holy Spirit, the Giver of Life, which are granted for the good of the Church, the Body of Christ, for building up the Community, and for serving the Church.

Summary

Dimensions of Sophia

The Created Sophia
- The Cosmic Sophia (as World Spirit)
- Sophia in the Economy of Salvation = the people of Israel
- The Icon of Sophia = Maria
- Sophia as the Mystical Body of Christ = The Church
- The Apocalyptic, Eschatological Sophia

The Uncreated Sophia
- The Logos
- The Holy Spirit as Mother

Aspect of the Essence of God

Concerning "the maternal face of God" there is a consensus today in the Catholic Church, that the essence of God (the "One God") has both paternal and maternal properties, because He is the "absolute Being," the totality of being and life, the first cause and template of creatures and so of maternity and femininity too.

The source of that can be the text of Genesis 1:27: "God created mankind in his image; in the image of God he created them; male and female he created them." Thus in God is (or may be) present the masculine and feminine character! God is a spiritual being and does not have a body, thus this character is not equivalent to human sexuality, but only an analogically, symbolically understood masculinity and femininity (or paternality and maternality).

Aspect of the Persons in the Holy Trinity

On the basis of our journey in sophiology we can draw up only possibilities and suppositions, not certainties:

1. Polarities permeate nature, man and all levels of being, and this suggests a nuptial structure of being that may hold true even for God, the Absolute Being (the *Esse Ipsum*).

2. Ancient philosophies lead us to the concept of Logos-Sophia or the organizing principle of the world. This concept appears in ancient Greek literature as well.

3. From the forgotten pages of the Old Testament, from the Wisdom literature, the figure of Hokmah-Sophia or Divine Wisdom takes shape, who is a personal reality, feminine and maternal in character, and who has a cosmological and ethical role.

4. The minimalist Jewish and Christian traditions regard Sophia as a divine substance in which case, according to the Christian concept, she achieves personal traits in the Holy Trinity (viz. Bulgakov).

5. According to a more general conviction, her apparent personal and maternal features show that she takes part in creation (*arche*, consultant and coworker of Yahweh). She is the World-Soul because her dress is the world and she is personalized in the people of Israel. The same features are attributed to Shekinah in Jewish literature after the Old Testament. *The Old Testament* also reports on the bridal relation of Yahweh and Sophia.

6. In Philo's religious thoughts Sophia is a central figure. She is the daughter of Yahweh, the idea of ideas, the mother of Logos. Philo did not equate Sophia with Logos as it was mistakenly supposed.

7. Many Christian thinkers attribute a mariological and/or theological role to Sophia of the Old Testament beyond her cosmological role (*arche*).

8. Sophia is also present in the New Testament as the cosmic dimension of salvation: she is the wisdom embodied in Mary, the human nature of Christ; she is the mystical body of Christ and will be present at the end of time. Created Sophia is the daughter of the Father, companion of Logos in creation, and the image of the Holy Spirit.

9. According to iconographic representations and according to many mystics, the cosmic-aeonian Sophia is embodied in Mary;

this condition was her kenosis but it is with the Assumption of Mary that Sophia's being is fulfilled.

10. The Church Fathers accepted the notion of created Sophia, together with her cosmic, mariological, and theological features and they accepted the notion of non-created Sophia as well, whom they identify with either the Logos or the Holy Spirit.

11. In the liturgy of the Eastern churches and especially in the Palamite tradition, Sophia's presence is significant. Here the mariological dimension becomes dominant and, for the first time, the idea of the divine nuptial is expressed either in the relation of the Father and Sophia-Mary or of Logos and Mary. Naturally, this nuptial is never biological; it is always existential.

12. This tradition is followed by Russian religious thought in the nineteenth century, but Sophia's cosmic dimension is also emphasized and here appears the idea that Sophia is the icon of the Holy Spirit. Sophia becomes a favorite figure of Russian church ornaments and iconography: the icons often depict her cosmic features in the form of an angel.

13. Similar inroads have been explored by visionaries and mystics of the Western tradition, especially Hildegard of Bingen, who believes that Sophia represents the Holy Spirit. The Holy Spirit–Sophia–Mary–Church equation is attested to by paintings and pictures as well.

14. In the sophiology of Jakob Boehme, out of *Ungrund* or the primary source of being springs the spiritual, maternal companion of the Father, the non-created Wisdom, and their fruit is the Son.

15. On the basis of the above, sophiology (Sophia and teachings about her) can be approached with religious, philosophical, and scientific views alike and thus it is universally part of human consensus.

16. According to a widespread opinion, created Sophia or World-Soul (and thus Mary) does not form a hypostatic unity with the Holy Spirit as opposed to the embodied Logos; rather, she is only an image, a created reflection or a projection of the Holy Spirit.

17. On the other hand, many people accept that the divine nuptial (self-denial, gift-giving, starting new life without any carnal aspects)

is present in the life of the Holy Trinity: in the relation of the Father and the Holy Spirit (*ad intra*) and in creation in the pair of Logos and Sophia and, furthermore, in salvation in the relation of Christ and Mary and of Christ and the Church (*ad extra*).

18. Sporadically the idea appears that the Holy Spirit–World-Soul–Sophia–Mary logical series is just as valid as the Logos–cosmic Logos–embodied Logos (Christ) derivation, but, of course, according to theology, Mary is not the incarnation of the Spirit.

19. In this system of coordinates the relation of Sophia and Logos is a mother-son relation on all levels (immanent Trinity, creation, embodiment) and not a sacred marriage.

20. If the latter is true, the consequence might appear to be that the Mother of God is also a Mother-God (like the Holy Spirit), an embodied divine person; however, this idea, that Mary would be an incarnation of the Spirit, has been consistently rejected by both the Eastern and the Western Churches.

21. Beyond reviewing traditional approaches the most significant discovery of a new sophiology could be the recognition of the Holy Spirit as the *representative of the feminine in the Divine Being.*

22. According to the teachings of Syriac theology, "it seems rather encouraging for pneumatology that in the Study of Creation, Mercy, and the Church *we can call the Spirit the Mother of Creation, the Mother of the Recreated, and the Mother of the Church.*"[1]

23. This is the maternity of the Spirit in the Economy of Salvation, but—according to the identity of the external and internal Trinity—it leads us to the notion of the eternal maternity of the Spirit as well.

24. The phrase "in the Arche was the Logos" (John 1:1) according to some people also expresses that the Logos hides from eternity in the Holy Spirit as in a maternal womb.

25. The greeting of the angel (Luke 1:35), as a "temporal" event, perhaps, can be also an expression of the eternal bearing of the Son from the Spirit-Mother.

1. *Dogmatics* I, 542.

Summary

26. The maternity as locution or symbol is here only for comparison, an appropriation of the Divine "maternal character" to the Spirit.

27. The maternity of the Spirit naturally is not exclusive. The Spirit has "a hundred faces," in the words of Henri Boulad,[2] and its mystery is incomprehensible to us.

28. Some people may be afraid that the femininity of the Spirit leads to a "tritheism" (polytheism). I would ask them if three male divine persons do not lead to that as well? Of course not—the three persons possess the same divine nature (essence, being). Even if the Holy Spirit has maternal characteristics, she still receives the "one essence."

29. *If* the maternity of the Spirit proves to be true, this may lead to a *hieros gamos* of the Father and the Spirit-Mother (of which fruit is the Son). This *archetype* may be the template and source of all dualities and triads of created things and the unity of man and woman.

On the basis of sophian pneumatology we can avoid the pitfalls of the errors regarding sexuality (homosexuality, transsexuality, polygamy, etc.) or that of feminism and gender ideology and we can conserve the dignity and beauty of the family, which is constructed on the duality and unity of the love community of man and woman as the *definitive image and likeness of God*, viz. of the Holy Trinity.

This new sophiology and its pneumatological flourishing may have a far-reaching effect on our (a little) patriarchal theology, on our social convictions, and on our common views on man, and it may transform our relationship with the created world and lead to a new, sophianic mentality in various scientific areas.

---

2. Henri Boulad, *A Szentlélek ezer arca / The hundred faces of Holy Spirit* (Budapest: Kairosz, 2005), 195.

Appendix

I. The Miniature of Codex Syriacus

II. Sapientia in the Missal of Hildesheim

III. 2nd Vision of Hildegard of Bingen: Hakmoth Yahweh

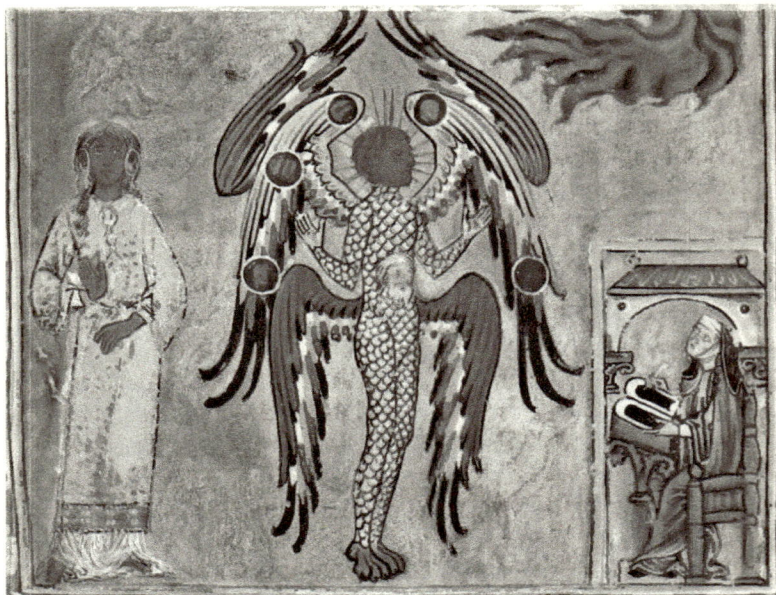

IV. 9th Vision of Hildegard of Bingen

V. 1st Vision of Hildegard of Bingen:
Wisdom with the Lamb

VI. Throne Companion of Yahweh

VII. Jan van Eyck: The Central Board of the Altar in Ghent

VIII. Michelangelo: The Creation of Man (detail)
in the Sistine Chapel

Appendix

IX. Matthias Grünewald: Tabernacle of the Altar of Isenheim

X. Fresco from the Church of Ingolstadt

XI. The Teaching Board of the Loreto-Church in Birkenstein

XII. Trinity-Icon from 19th-Century Russia

XIII. Trinity-Icon of Andrei Rublev

XIV. Trinity-Icon of Theophanes the Greek

ОБА СОФІИ ПРЕМУДРОСТИ БОЖІЕИ.

XV. Sophia-Icon in Novgorod

XVI. Sophia-Icon of Stroganoff

XVII. Apse of the Sophia Cathedral in Kiev

XVIII. The Holy Trinity from Urschalling

XIX. Dietric Bouts: The Crowning of Mary

XX. Mother-Earth, 20ᵗʰ-Century Romanian Painting

Bibliography

A dogmatika kézikönyve [A Handbook of Dogmatics]. Budapest: Vigilia, 1996.

Algermissen, Konrad. *Konfessionskunde*. Paderborn: Bonifacius Druckerei, 1969.

Allen, Paul M. *Vladimir Soloviev: Russian Mystic*. Hudson: SteinerBooks, 1978.

Andreev, Daniel. *The Rose of the World*. Hudson: Lindisfarne Press, 1997.

Argüelles, Miriam and José. *Weiblich weit wie der Himmel*. Haldenwang: Irisiana Verlag, 1979.

Aurobindo, Sri. *Die Mutter*. Zürich: Rascher, 1945.

Backofen, Johann Jakob. *Das Mutterrecht*. Frankfurt: Suhrkamp, 1978.

Bargatsky, Walter. *Das Universum lebt: Die aufsehenerregende Hypothese vom organischen Aufbau des Weltalls*. München: Heine, 1978.

Barnay, Sylvie. *La Vierge: Femme au visage divine*. Paris: Gallimard, 2000.

Bateson, Gregory. *Ökologie des Geistes*. Frankfurt: Suhrkamp, 1983.

Bazner, Erhard. *Die Naturgeister*. München: Drei Eichen Verlag, 1967.

Beinert, Wolfgang. "Die mariologischen Dogmen und ihre Entfaltung." In *Handbuch der Marienkunde*, 232–314. Regensburg: Pustet, 1984.

Bocjanovskij, Vladimir F. *Bogoiskateli*. Petersburg-Moscow, 1911.

Borne, Gerhard von dem. *Der Gral in Europa, Wurzeln und Wirkungen*. Stuttgart: Urachhaus, 1976.

Brockmöllet, Klemens. *Christentum am Morgen des Atomzeitalters*. Frankfurt: Knecht, 1955.

Brugger, Walter. *Philosophisches Wörterbuch*. Freiburg: Herder, 1976.

Bühlmann, Walbert. *Alle haben denselben Gott*. Frankfurt: Knecht, 1978.

Bulgakov, Sergei. *Sophia, the Wisdom of God: An Outline of Sophiology*. New York: Lindisfarne Press, 1993.

Cioran, Samuel David. *The Apocalyptic Symbolism of Andrej Belyj*. Paris: The Hague, 1973.

———. *Vladimir Solov'ev and the Knighthood of the Divine Sophia*. Ontario: Wilfrid Laurier University Press, 1977.

Cselényi, István. *La revisione dell' essere*. Vaticano: SITA, 2001.

———. "Risposta di San Tommaso d'Aquino al problema dell'essere dell'uomo modern." In *Atti del Congresso Internazionale su l'umanesimo cristiano nel III millennio: la prospettiva di Tommaso d'Aquino,* *Vol. II.* 246–60.Vaticano: SITA, 2005.

Dahm, Helmut. *Vladimir Soloviev and Max Scheler: Attempt at a Comparative Interpretation. A Contribution to the History of Phenomenology.* Boston: Dordrecht, 1975.

Daniélou, Jean. *Platonisme et Theologie mystique.* Paris: Cerf, 1954.

Eberz, Offried. *Sophia und Logos.* München: Selbstverlag Luzia Eberz, 1980.

Eliade, Mircea and Joseph M. Kitigawa. *Grundfragen der Religionswissenschaft.* Salzburg: Otto Müller, 1963.

Eliade, Mircea. *Geschichte der religiösen Ideen.* Freiburg: Herder 1981.

Ernst, Robert. *Maria: die sichtbare Gestalt des Hl. Geistes.* Eupen: Markus-Verlag, 1955.

Frieda, Betty. *Der Weiblichkeitswahn oder die Selbstbefreiung der Frau, Ein Emanzipationskonzept.* Hamburg: Rowohlt, 1970.

Golowin, Sergius. *Die weisen Frauen.* Basel: Sphinx, 1982.

Gould, Emily. *Am Anfang war die Frau.* Münschen: Verlag Frauenoffensive, 1980.

Gutting, Ernst. *Offensive gegen den Patriarchalismus.* Freiburg: Herder, 1987.

Jung, Carl Gustav. *Animus und Anima,* Zürich 1974.

———. *Die Archetypen des kollektiven Unbewussten.* Olten, 1976.

Küng, Hans. *Die Frau im Christentum.* München: Piper Verlag, 2001.

Mack, Burton Lee. *Logos und Sophia: Untersuchungen zur Weiheitstheologie im hellenistischen Judentum.* Göttingen: Vandenhoeck & Ruprecht, 1975.

Martin, Michael. *The Submerged Reality: Sophiology and the Turn to a Poetic Metaphysics.* Kettering: Angelico Press, 2015.

Philo. "Quaestiones in Genesim." In *Ebrietate* 31.

———. *De ebrietate (A mámorról).*

———. *De somniis.*

———. *Fuga.*

Powell, Robert. *The Christ Mystery.* Fair Oaks: Rudolf Steiner College Press, 1999).

———. *Christian Hermetic Astrology.* Hudson: Anthroposophic Press, 1998.

———. *Chronicle of the Living Christ. The Life and Ministry of Jesus Christ: Foundations of Cosmic Christianity.* Hudson: Anthroposophic Press, 1996.

Bibliography

————. *Cosmic Aspects of the Foundation Stone*. Great Barrington: Golden Stone Press, 1990.

————. *Divine Sophia, Holy Wisdom*. Nicasio: Sophia Foundation of North America, 1997.

————. *The Sign of the Son of Man in the Heavens: Sophia and the New Star Wisdom*. Vancouver: Sun Cross Press, 1999.

————. *The Most Holy Trinosophia and the New Revelations of the Divine Feminine*. Great Barrington: Anthroposophic Press, 2000.

Scheja, Georg. *Der Isenheimer Altar des Matthias Grünewald*. Köln: DuMont Schauberg, 1969.

Schipflinger, Thomas. *Sophia–Maria: Eine Ganzheitliche Vision der Schöpfung*. München–Zürich: Verlag Neue Stadt, 1988.

Siebel, Wigand. *Der heilige Geist als Relation: Eine soziale Trinitätslehre*. Münster: Herder, 1986.

Slesinski, Robert. *Pavel Florensky: A Metaphysics of Love*. Crestwood: St.Vladimir's Seminary Press, 1984.

Spenneut, Michael. "Le stoicisme des Peres de l'Eglise." In *Patristica Sorbonnensia*, Paris: Cerf, 1957.

Steiner, Rudolf. *Ancient Myths and the New Isis Mystery*. Hudson: Anthroposophic Press, 1992.

————. *Bilder okkulter Siegel und Schule*. Dornach: Rudolf Steiner Verlag, 1977.

————. *The Being of Anthroposophy*. Hudson: Anthroposophic Press, 1997.

Stone, Merlin. *When God was a Woman*. New York: Amazon, 1976.

Talmud: Der babylonische Talmud. Ausgewählt, übersetzt und erklärt von Reinhold Mayer. München: Goldmann, 1963.

Teilhard de Chardin, Pierre. *Az emberi jelenség*. Budapest: Gondolat Kiadó, 1973.

————. *Hymne an das Ewig-Weibliche*, Kommentar von H. Lubac. Einsiedeln: Johannes Verlag, 1968.

Tüttő, George, *Femininity in the Holy Trinity and in our World*. Essex: McCrimmon Publishing Company, 2004.

Wellek, Albert. *Die Polarität im Aufbau des Charakters*. Bern und München: Francke Verlag, 1966.

"Zu den Begriffen Personifikation, Hypostase und Person." In *Wörterbuch der Religionen*. Ed. A. Bertholet. Stuttgart: Urchhaus, 1976.

www.ingramcontent.com/pod-product-compliance
Lightning Source LLC
Chambersburg PA
CBHW032050080426
42733CB00006B/223